*"I prefer endorsements by unfamous nameless, no-name, noteless, obscure, uncelebrated, unknown, unrecognized, and unsung . . .
sweet friends, real people who actually know me."*
—**Victorya Wright**

"Although God works in each of our lives in more or less obvious and unique ways, Victorya is blessed with that special sense of recognition that enables her to see His hand as He is doing it. Most of us are not attuned or observant enough to see His story . . . shame on us! How much richer our Christian lives and our testimonies would be if we practiced what Victorya does and developed a significant ability to be conscious of the times the Lord is directing something exciting and unique in our own circumstances."

—**Gail Stewart**, *USAF veteran; retired from Mocksville Police Department, Mocksville, North Carolina*

—**Gordon Stewart**, *USAF retired; former administrator of The Julian Center, Julian, California*

"The collection of Victorya's God experiences is heartwarming and touching. I learned a number of things: God is still in the business of miracles; we can trust Him because He is a faithful and loving God; we know He will hear us and He will answer our prayers. His grace and mercy give us hope and we are blessed beyond measure. Thanks, my friend, for sharing your stories."

—**Genie Summers**, *retired kindergarten teacher, friend, sister in Christ*

"'Vickie' Wright navigates life as a God-follower with intrepid faith, recognizing that God orchestrates every personal and unique circumstance of her life whether good, bad, or hard. A random encounter in an obscure café in Europe, for example, turns out to be a divine appointment, a special God-story. Her stories are amazing, but true. If you've ever wanted to be more aware of how God is directing every detail of life, read this book. It will open your eyes to see God at work authoring your own God-stories."

—**Gwen Counts,** *long-time friend and fellow God-follower; Director, Coastal Carolina Center for Women's Ministries*

"As a mother, grandmother, and educator in early childhood education, I have found that sharing our narratives is an important way of expressing our identity in Christ.

To the cherished readers of Victorya's remarkable book, detailing her encounters with God, I hope you find encouragement in the vastness of our Heavenly Father's presence in every situation. May He bring unexpected joy into your journey with Him. God is always purposeful in leading us to extraordinary moments of divine appointment."

—**Sydney Burris,** *Sister in Christ and friend*

"This book is a must read whether you question your faith, or your relationship with God is strong. Victorya's God stories are a testament that there is always a plan, even if we cannot see it, are lost searching for answers, or think we have it all figured out. God will lead you exactly to where you need to go. For me it was meeting Victorya 8.5 years ago [2016] on a beach! Her testimonies turned my own 'coincidences' into God guided paths and I hope they do the same for those who read this book!"

—**Taylor Scott,** *God Story Participant, Bonus Daughter, Lifelong seeker of God*

"Victorya has been in my life for almost 40 years. We have lived life together as young homeschool moms, survived through parenting teens, children getting married and we now continue and as true Doppelgänger friends. I can attest to the true life stories in Victorya's book, *God Stories*. It has inspired me to search and be aware of how God shows up in everyday life. I have discovered my own God stories, that I would not have been aware of before reading her book. After hearing her *God stories* over the years, I was glad to see them come to print. She uses her real stories to tell how God has purpose in the little things, both the 'accidental' things, and the big things that happen in our lives. You will see how much He shows up when you read through each story.

Victorya gives all of us encouragement to be aware of our own story and purpose that will ultimately bring us closer to our own relationship with God. We won't be just living our daily life, unaware of the stories, but her stories will open our eyes to look and remember."

—**Dawn Todd,** *Wife, Mother of 4, Grandmother of 18, Owner of The Original Swab Company*

"I wish I had recorded the *God Storys* Victorya has told me over the years. Some of them have helped me to see God's sense of humor and made me laugh out loud. His *God Storys* are a deep expression of who Victorya is and her walk with the Lord. May you be blessed as much as I have been to hear these stories throughout the years . . ."

—**Jacqueline Claudin,** *manicurist, friend, sister in Christ*

"Dear Victorya. Thanks for your message. We read the two chapters with much interest and respect. Your writing is fine, and your experiences described there are intriguing. We remember you as a friendly, generous, honest and positive-thinking lady. Now the book confirms our initial impression. Good luck with your future travels."

—**Gideon* and Neta Aran,** **Dept. of Sociology & Anthropology, The Hebrew University, Jerusalem, Israel*

"'Brunei … where's that?' While this might be a typical comment one hears, an initial trip to the little nation of Brunei Darussalam, with Victorya and her family in 1999, certainly put Brunei onto the map for them. And not just onto their map, but into their hearts. For 25 years now, Victorya has lived and breathed Brunei, albeit she has only actually visited the nation once … but that was enough, together with a timely relationship she has since developed with a Bruneian medical healthcare worker. Few have visited Brunei, even though it is an absolutely delightful place … a history born out of folklore, its capital city includes a 500 year-old village set right in the middle of the river, a skyline dotted with more golden domes than one can count, the largest royal palace in the world, local women who love to dress in the most colorful sarong kebaya, a local population who enjoy free education and healthcare and no income tax thanks to the nation's rich reserves of oil and gas and the generous ruling Sultan, yet at the same time Brunei is a strictly Islamic nation. The wonderful thing is, God is writing HIS story in Brunei, too. Victorya and her family speak of the privilege of 'getting in on what God is doing there.' Brunei, however, is only one part of Victorya's story … in fact, her life is full of God stories, and you will be excited to 'get in on these' as she shares them here."

—**Brian Newton,** *Missions Mobilizer with OMF International (retired)*

GOD STORYS

TOLD BY A DAUGHTER *of the* MOST HIGH KING

VICTORYA WRIGHT

CLAY BRIDGES
PRESS

God Storys: Told By a Daughter of the Most High King
Copyright © 2025 by Victorya Wright
Published by Clay Bridges Press in Houston, TX
www.ClayBridgesPress.com

All rights reserved. No part of this publication may be reproduced, stored in a retrieval system, or transmitted in any form by any means, electronic, mechanical, photocopy, recording, or otherwise, without the prior permission of the publisher, except as provided for by USA copyright law.

Unless otherwise indicated, scripture quotations are taken from the Holy Bible, New International Version®, NIV®. Copyright ©1973, 1978, 1984, 2011 by Biblica, Inc.™ Used by permission of Zondervan. All rights reserved worldwide. www.zondervan.com The "NIV" and "New International Version" are trademarks registered in the United States Patent and Trademark Office by Biblica, Inc.™

Scripture quotations Marked (ESV) are taken from the ESV® Holy Bible, English Standard Version®), copyright © 2001 by Crossway, a publishing ministry of Good News Publishers. Used by permission. All rights reserved.

Scripture quotations marked (KJV) are taken from the King James Version (KJV): King James Version, public domain.

Scripture quotations marked (MSG) are taken from THE MESSAGE, copyright © 1993, 2002, 2018 by Eugene H. Peterson. Used by permission of NavPress. All rights reserved. Represented by Tyndale House Publishers, Inc.

ISBN: 978-1-68488-137-6 (Paperback)
ISBN: 978-1-68488-139-0 (Hardback)
eISBN: 978-1-68488-138-3

Special Sales: Most Clay Bridges titles are available in special quantity discounts. Custom imprinting or excerpting can also be done to fit special needs. Contact Clay Bridges at Info@ClayBridgesPress.com

SPECIAL NOTE

You may have noticed the spelling of the word STORYS in this book. The author and publisher know that the correct spelling of this word is STORIES, but the author believes with all sincerity that the Lord, through prayer, gave her this spelling, and therefore has purpose in it.

Disclaimer: To protect the privacy of individuals, some names and identifying details have been changed.

Any websites, email addresses, or resources mentioned in this book are accurate at the time of publication. The author reserves the right to modify or discontinue these at their sole discretion, without notice.

Want to connect with the author?
Website: www.godstorys.com
Email: Victorya@Godstorys.com
Postal: God Storys by Victorya
P O Box 2166
Carlsbad, CA 92018

Dedicated to my faithful prayer partners who lovingly prodded and encouraged me to report these God storys for His glory and for your encouragement.

Bear one another's burdens and so fulfil the law of Christ. For if anyone thinks he is something when he is nothing he deceives himself.

—Galatians 6:2–3 ESV

TABLE OF CONTENTS

Introduction	1
Cathy	5
Janet	11
Katherine	17
Brunei	21
Rosie	33
Joi	39
Adam	41
Jenna	45
Family Tsunami	47
Wake Up	51
Dawn	53
Madison	57
Tonya	61
Snakes	65
Train Angel	75
Makeover	81
Not Alone	87
The Ticket	95
Noy	99

Christine	105
Gabrielle	111
Israel	125
Jack	131
Taylor	143
Calabria	147
Wait	157
Crash	159
Theodore	161
PREQUEL: Fred and Marilyn	167
Why Victorya?	173
Endnotes	175

INTRODUCTION

I have been asked, "What is the purpose of this book? I believe that the answer to that question lies in the fact that you are holding this book in your hands and reading these God storys. That is not a coincidence; it is another God incidence. I do not believe in coincidence. I believe that our lives and our world are beautifully orchestrated by a very personal, very relational Creator.

In a recent sermon, a young preacher who was filling in for his father preached about Jonah. He mentioned that our purpose here on planet Earth is to pursue a relationship with God and to proclaim what He has done. As I listened, I realized that this message reflected my own experiences with the God who breathed life into my nostrils seventy-two years ago.

Even as a young child, I had memorable encounters with God. Initially, I was too young to attribute those encounters to Him, but as I learned to recognize His inaudible voice, His quiet whispers, His presence, His nudges, His directing me, His "God Taps," my relationship with Him deepened, and I thoroughly enjoyed proclaiming what He had done. If you are a believer, I pray that these God storys will encourage you and deepen your relationship with Him. If you are not a believer, I pray that you will see Him differently after you encounter Him as One who is intentionally personal and interested in you as a unique individual.

After all, we are created in His image and likeness. That alone makes us incredibly special. [Enjoy listening to the song, The Truth by Megan Woods]

This book is not about me; it is not about spiritual one-upmanship. I do not embrace experiential Christianity alone but acknowledge the importance of knowing and studying Scripture as an essential component to deepening our understanding of God. This book is all about Him . . . about having a relationship with Him. I am an ordinary person; I am an ordinary Christian. I am merely His scribe writing out of obedience to Him.

Many years ago, God revealed to me through His love, provision, and involvement that I have His favor even though my life has not been without difficulties, trials, and challenges. I have grown to embrace suffering, even savor it. I have gratitude for my trials, for I know they have purpose, which is to make me more like Him, so that He is glorified. As you read about the great, yet ordinary, things that He has done, I hope that you will be filled with a new sense of awe and wonder. I pray that you will be filled with praise and gratitude, for He is worthy to be praised.

I caution you not to attempt to replicate my relationship with Him but to actively and intentionally pursue your own relationship with Him. A relationship with God is built the way you build a relationship with any other person who is also created in His image and likeness. Spend time with Him, listening, reading, and studying His love letters and expectations in the Scriptures; talking to Him; and being still in His presence.

I cling to the certainty that there is absolutely nothing more exciting that being a Christian . . . being in relationship with the God who breathed life into my nostrils.

> *The LORD has done great things for us, and we are filled with joy.*
>
> —Psalm 126:3

INTRODUCTION

And the Lord *God formed man of the dust of the ground, and* **breathed into his nostrils the breath of life**; *and man became a living soul.*
—Genesis 2:7–9 KJV (emphasis added)

Worship the Lord *in the splendor of holiness.*
—Psalm 96:9 ESV

Oh, sing to the Lord *a new song. Sing to the* Lord *all the earth. Sing to the* Lord*, bless his name; tell of his salvation from day to day. Declare his glory among the nations, his marvelous works among all the peoples. For great is the* Lord*, and greatly to be praised; he is to be feared above all gods. For all the gods of the peoples are worthless idols, but the* Lord *made the heavens. Splendor and majesty are before him; strength and beauty are in his sanctuary. Ascribe to the* Lord*, O families of the peoples, ascribe to the* Lord *glory and strength! Ascribe to the* Lord *the glory due his name; bring an offering, and come into his courts! Worship the* Lord *in the splendor of holiness; tremble before him, all the earth. Say among the nations, "The* Lord *reigns! Yes, the world is established; it shall never be moved; he will judge the peoples with equity." Let the heavens be glad, and let the earth rejoice; let the sea roar, and all that fills it; let the field exult, and everything in it! Then shall all the trees of the forest sing for joy before the* Lord*, for he comes to judge the earth. He will judge the world in righteousness, and the peoples in his faithfulness.*
—Psalm 96:1–13 ESV

The Israelites erected standing stones to remember God's mighty acts; the Bible mentions standing stones in several places, including Genesis 35, Exodus 24, Joshua 4, and Deuteronomy 16. *God Storys* is my standing stone to remember and proclaim what God has done in my life!

CATHY

My cousin Rosie left me to return to Santa Cruz, leaving me in the guest house to start formulating my thoughts and organizing them to begin writing. Even though for years I had no intention of writing these God Storys, I had kept a list of them in the notepad of my phone. When I sat down to organize my thoughts, I created a single sticky note for every God story that I felt directed to proclaim. By midafternoon, I started feeling paralysis set in. I felt completely overwhelmed as to how I would ever be able to relay all these stories in a way that would benefit and encourage people and give God glory. I sent out prayer requests, asking for help with the overwhelming feeling of paralysis. I received wonderful supportive and encouraging prayers, but one in particular really helped me.

Cathy and her husband Greg currently live in Rock Hill, South Carolina. When I first met her in 1985, they lived in Carlsbad, California. My husband at the time and I lived in Wrightwood, California, in the San Bernadino mountains. I had grown up never wanting any children. I was the oldest of four in a family that went through a terrible divorce when I was twelve. As the oldest child, I had too many responsibilities for a twelve-year-old. My husband at the time really wanted a child. As a Christian wife, I felt that it was my responsibility to submit to that. We tried and tried to conceive with no success. Being the research person that I am, I began looking for the most highly recommended infertility specialist in the area where we were living. After a year of expensive, embarrassing, and sometimes painful infertility tests, the infertility specialist informed us that we both had insurmountable infertility and would never conceive. Quite frankly, I was not unhappy about the news. I was hoping to go to graduate school. However, God had different plans for us. We soon learned that contrary to the infertility test results shared at that consultation, I was already pregnant with our firstborn!

On the delivery table, the infertility specialist announced, "Enjoy her; she is the only one you will ever have." Seventeen months later, our second child, our firstborn son, was born. Over the years, many people have said, "Oh you had a really bad doctor." But I know in my heart that is not true because I had researched and found the best specialist. In reality, I have a really big God with a really big sense of humor. Since then, God blessed us with seven pregnancies and five live births. We have two adult daughters and three adult sons. Four of our children are married, and four of them have children.

But this story goes back to our firstborn, our oldest daughter. I had not anticipated being pregnant or having a baby, and I was ill-prepared. To my recollection, I had only held one baby in my entire life, and that was my girlfriend's baby girl. After our daughter was born, I took six weeks of maternity leave, which turned into three months of acute colic and sleepless nights, I realized that there was no way that I could go back to work and leave my baby girl with someone to watch her during the day. So that began a journey to figure out how I could be a stay-at-home mom. At the time, my income as a dental hygienist was double what my husband's income was. So my not going back to work meant that we had to get very creative to live on a budget that was less than half the income we were accustomed to living on. We sold our A-frame loft cabin in the woods in Wrightwood, California, and then proceeded to look for a place to live where the rent was no more than $350 a month, which was all we could budget for housing.

That seemed like an impossible task. Where on earth would we be able to live as a family of three in Southern California in 1985 for $350 a month? But God had that already worked out. We had a family friend named Anne who was in a women's Bible study, and she reported to us that a woman in her Bible study, Cathy, had sold a home and bought a new home, but the original sale had fallen through because when buyers discovered that the house had been built on a landfill, they backed out of the sales; that happened seven times. Anne introduced us to Cathy and her husband Greg who were willing to rent us their beautiful home with a three-car garage, a gazebo, and a spa in the backyard in Oceanside, California, for $350 month until the house could finally be sold. That was the means that God used to move us to San Diego, California.

In the weeks and months that followed, Cathy and I became very good friends, sisters in the Lord. Forty years later and with 3,000 miles separating us, we remain dear friends and prayer partners. Cathy's parents, Chip and Marge, moved from Long Island, New York, to Oceanside, to be closer to their daughter and grandchildren. Chip and Marge became the grandparents to our children that our children did not have.

Eventually, Cathy and Greg relocated to South Carolina for Greg's work, and her parents soon followed. Yesterday, while writing and feeling overwhelmed as if I had been given an impossible task to accomplish, I was empowered when I opened my text messages and read Cathy's words of encouragement:

> My precious friend, you are going to encounter great spiritual warfare because the enemy does not want you to proclaim God's goodness and faithfulness in your life. As a read this paraphrase on Psalm 71 this morning, I thought it would encourage you. This was my mom's

book, *Psalms Now*, I am using it in my devotions. Remember that He is greater in you than He who is in this world. I am continuing to be in the battle with you. Lift me up to the throne of Grace also.

The excerpt from her mom's devotional for today reads:

"Good Lord, You have kept me within the secure embrace of Your love these many years. My life is one long list of divine deliverances. I have come running to you again and again when the forces of evil set themselves against me. From the moment of my birth, I was dedicated to Your will, given life by You, only to yield it back to You. And since that time, the days and hours of my life have been filled with praise for You. But the enemies that plagued me in my youth still lay siege to my soul, looking for chinks in my armor, for loopholes in my defenses through which to enter and lay waste. Now as I near the late afternoon and evening of my life, I continue to seek Your love and mercy. Even while I shout Your praises and proclaim Your salvation, I reach for the assurance of Your love and concern. You have guided me through my precarious youth, now I need your grace for my senior years. Fill my heart with purpose and my mouth with praises so that I may continue to proclaim Your name and Your salvation to all who will listen. You are, oh God, the Creator and Performer of great and glorious things. There is no one like You. You have kept me safe throughout life's conflicts, led me through its crucible of experiences, drawn me back from its pitfalls and precipices, healed my wounds, and comforted me in my afflictions. Thus I know that You will continue to love and care for me. I will dedicate my remaining days to praising you and espousing Your faithfulness and proclaiming Your love and concern for all who will turn to You. May every fiber of my being and every activity of my life resound with praises to my God.¹"

When she penned that text and sent me a screenshot of those devotional pages, Cathy probably didn't know that was exactly what I needed to read and hear to move forward and be empowered to do this great work. Forty years ago, God put in place my friendship with Cathy, which led to her sending me those devotional pages yesterday to help me move forward today.

JANET

In 1991 I was pregnant with my fourth child, and it was a very difficult pregnancy. In the spring, I woke up on a Tuesday morning with my jaw completely locked closed. It was very painful. The dentist for whom I worked part time said it was the worst case he had ever seen. It took weeks of physical therapy for me to be able to open my mouth. Then I developed bilateral carpal tunnel syndrome and had to wear braces on both my hands and forearms. I was incapable of using my hands and wrists in many traditional ways. I could not work part time in the dental office. To make matters worse, I had borderline toxemia and gestational diabetes, and I was caring for three small children.

My oldest daughter was going to turn six years of age on her October birthday. I was of the mindset that we should wait as long as possible to put children into kindergarten, but legally, at six, she had to be enrolled. So, I started searching to see which kindergarten she should go to. One of my dental patients was a principal at the local Christian elementary school in Fallbrook. He suggested that I go to the school to observe the teachers, look at the curriculum, and see how the kindergarten classroom was run. I followed through on his recommendation, but I was not sold on that private Christian school for my daughter. I could not see a difference between the Christian school and the public schools. They both celebrated Halloween, and at the time that didn't make sense to me. I also went to two other public school kindergartens and was disappointed when I saw a poster of the Mexican president and the flag of Mexico but no evidence that I was in the United States. At the second school, while I was talking to a teacher during recess, I saw one student on top of another pummeling the student a short distance away. I pointed this out to the teacher, "Look, look, look . . . ," I said, but she just shrugged her shoulders and said, "Kids will be kids." I would not have been happy to have my daughter pummeled by another student. So, because of those two experiences at the public schools, I decided to enroll my daughter in the private Christian school. However, there was a waiting list.

In August 1991 my husband informed me that he was no longer going to be employed as a territory rep for the five Western States. He was suddenly unemployed. Because his company was located in Georgia, they had somehow finagled out of paying California unemployment insurance, and my husband found himself out of a job and out of income. This made it difficult to justify spending money we didn't have on private school tuition. So, God directed me to consider homeschooling my oldest daughter for kindergarten. I was not enthusiastic about it. At the time, I foolishly wanted my kids to grow up in the *real* world, whatever that means. Once again, I was resistant, but I didn't want to put my daughter in the public-school kindergarten, and I couldn't afford to pay tuition for the private Christian school. So, I relented and agreed to homeschool her for kindergarten . . . just for one year.

It was a very difficult time of unemployment; we literally had no money. It was unlikely that I would have ever considered homeschooling my children had the situation not been as dire as it was. For years I would say, "I am only homeschooling my children for one more year." About three years into homeschooling, God showed me the benefits and advantages of homeschooling our children. I was thankful that He had propelled me into it for I could see the benefits my children reaped and the relationships they built with each other and with their parents. I really appreciated having them learn in an environment that was not age- or grade-segregated. I began to see traditional elementary school as a basic math problem. How many hours a day would other teachers influence my children, and how many hours of the day would we influence them? With God's direction and His constant support and provision, after twenty-eight years of home education, or what we called "parent taught" school, we graduated our youngest daughter from homeschool high school. Our five children were educated at home from kindergarten through high school, and I am happy to report they are all God-fearing, successful college graduates.

Now back to the time of unemployment and no income. It was a time that I would never have raised my hand and volunteered for, but it would have been tragic to miss that faith-building season of our lives.

Mary Flo and Bob held the mortgage to our home. They were the previous owners of the house and chose to be our lending bank. When we encountered this time of unemployment, they volunteered to refinance our loan for a lower interest rate and allowed us to pay interest-only payments until we got on our feet. That kept us from losing our house. One month we received an unexpected IRS tax refund check in the mailbox that was exactly enough to cover our mortgage payment for that month. Over and over again, God creatively provided for us in ways that we had no way of anticipating.

In November 1991, our fourth child (our third son) was born. Having had babies already, I knew within days that there was something very, very wrong with my baby boy. I took him back to the family doctor and said, "There is something wrong with my son, and I am not leaving here until you find out what it is." He tried to console me with, "Oh, he's just fine. You're probably going through some postpartum depression." But I insisted that he reexamine him and told him I wasn't leaving. He would have to call the police to remove me. He humored me and did another exam only days after my son's birth. To his surprise his man-sized pinkie penetrated the hole in my son's groin. We were immediately referred to Children's Hospital for my baby boy to have bilateral hernia surgery when he was only days old. I remember the pediatric surgeon asking our permission to surgically investigate both sides because frequently hernias are bilateral, and a second surgery would be needed if they didn't repair both sides the first time. We gave him permission and yes, our son had hernias on both sides, and the side that was less detectable was worse than the other side. To this day, he has internal surgical screens where the hernias had been.

It was almost Christmastime, but we were not planning to have a tree that year because we could not afford one. But our family friends, John and Anne, purchased and delivered a live tree to us so we would be able to have one that season.

A neighbor up the street who was a fireman, showed up on a Sunday morning delivering a shirt box with cookies in it. I remember having a bad attitude, thinking, "Great! That's what we really need . . . cookies!" And then I was terribly convicted when under the wax paper, under the cookies, I found cash! It was enough cash to meet our financial obligations that day.

But by far the most dramatic and memorable of all these provisions from the Lord came from Janet and Tim. I had been attending Bible Study Fellowship, and a woman named Janet was in my small group. She was also a homeschool mom with young children. We were not particularly good friends and quite honestly, I didn't really like her. She was a Birkenstock and denim skirt homeschool mom. I don't know exactly what that means, but I do know that at that time in my life, I did not want that stereotype for myself. It was a Sunday morning. My husband had taken our children to church, but I had stayed home with my baby boy who was recovering from bilateral hernia surgery. I got a phone call from Janet saying that she wanted to bring something by. As I recall, I had a bad attitude, thinking to myself, "Oh great, another box of cookies." But I told her that she could come by at any time.

Soon, I heard Janet and her husband Tim drive up about the same time that I heard my husband return from church with our children. So since I was bathing, dressing, and changing my baby boy's diaper, I was in no hurry to go out to greet Janet as I assumed that she was bringing another box or plate of Christmas cookies. When I finally got around to going out to the family room, I could not believe my eyes! Janet and her husband Tim had gone to Costco and purchased one of everything in Costco that was edible. Our family room floor was covered with food. There was everything from frozen pizzas to fifty-pound bags of beans and rice. I felt so embarrassed and so convicted by my terrible attitude. To this day I don't know whether that gift was just from Janet and Tim or whether they had gathered resources from other Christian friends. All I know is that without the delivery that day, I don't know how we would have fed our family of six as we did for the next *six months*. They brought enough food for us to eat for six months. After that, Janet became one of my dearest friends and prayer partners. She experienced her own health struggles, and we came alongside each other through some very difficult times. She passed to be with God forever on November 22, 2020. I miss her.

With my encouragement, my husband completed his master's degree in marriage and family therapy at Azusa Pacific University, but he had not yet taken his licensing exams. After nine months, his previous Georgia employer helped him find employment by mailing out his resumes. In April 1992, my husband took a job in a group home, a setting in which he had not previously worked. That job allowed him to get the required hours of supervision to be able to take his exams. When he was eligible, he passed his exams on the first attempt, becoming a licensed marriage and family therapist. With my God-given administration gifts, I opened two sole proprietor offices for him in two counties. That began his long and successful career as a mental health therapist.

God used that time of unemployment and almost no income to build my faith in Him. My relationship with God blossomed with those nine months of His unrequested and unrequired faithfulness. I trusted Him in a new way!

By the way . . . I now own and wear Birkenstocks too!

KATHERINE

Thirty years ago Katherine and I attended the same church in the little agricultural community of Fallbrook, California, in San Diego County. However, we did not know each other even though we attended the same church. Our church scheduled a weekend women's retreat in the local Ramona mountains. I do not remember why, but I was not interested in attending the retreat and as it turns out neither was Katherine. However, in God's sovereign plan, our husbands decided to encourage us to attend and, somewhat reluctantly, we both separately decided to go. When we arrived separately, everyone had already buddied up, and there was no one left to share a room with me except Katherine. Though neither of us had wanted to attend, we each thought, "Well, if I have to go, I can take off and have some time alone with the Lord, and that won't be such a bad thing."

So, that was the plan each of us had made before we arrived at the retreat center. The first night was for introductions and orientation, and it was announced that a mountain lion had been sighted on the retreat center grounds; therefore, no one was allowed to go outside alone, not even to the bathroom. Well unbeknownst to me, we were both heavyhearted about being stuck with each other. I was looking forward to having some alone time, and so was Katherine. So the next day, Saturday morning, instead of going to the group organized event, Katherine and I agreed to hike up to what we called "The Cross," which was a huge cross on top of the mountain. Hiking up the trail, we were two people who didn't know each other, who had never met before, who didn't want to be with each other, who really wanted to be alone. Katherine started talking; at one point, she looked at me and made this random statement that I will never forget: "If I had it to do over again, I would have homeschooled my kids." Well, that was the oddest and the most random comment, but the timing of it was incredible.

Katherine did not know that I had four children or that I was homeschooling them—one year at a time. I had gone into homeschooling kicking and screaming. (That is a different God Story for another time.) At the time, my youngest child, my third son, was three years old, and I was in the early stages of homeschooling early elementary for my two oldest children. What Katherine did not know was that I was very burned out, and I was considering quitting homeschooling. So when she blurted out her comment on our first day of getting to know one another on that hiking trail, I was shocked. I asked her why she would say something like that to me. She did not know anything about me! She did not know I had four children, and she did not know I was homeschooling.

The hike to The Cross that day was the beginning of a very special friendship. Katherine and I do not call each other BFFs, but we call each other YBFFAE, which means, "Your Best Friend Forever and Ever." Katherine and I are very different, but we share one thing in common. We both have a passion for the person of God, and we have a passion for His Word. Katherine has the largest servant's heart of any human being that I have ever met. Although her legal name is Mrs. Hawthorne, after that hike to The Cross, she became Aunt Katherine in our home and in our family. She was there for me as an overwhelmed parent with a lot of little kids. She would bring meals, and she would homeschool the kids when I couldn't get out of bed either because of migraines or other health issues or when I occasionally temped as a dental hygienist. I would leave behind lesson plans, and she would make sure they got done.

Without God's gift of Katherine in my life, I am convinced I would not have been able to complete the task of homeschooling five children from kindergarten through high school over a period of twenty-eight years. God knew I needed Katherine to help me accomplish His calling on my life and His plan for my children.

BRUNEI

When my oldest daughter and my oldest son were approaching sixth grade, I started planning what I was going to use for curriculum. As I had done every year of homeschooling, I tried to determine what would work best for our children for where they were at that time. Two curriculums caught my attention, but I was unusually indecisive about which curriculum to use. One curriculum, Liberty Press, was a very traditional textbook style in which they tested each student and customized a curriculum for them based on their test results. The other curriculum, Sonlight, was out of my comfort level; it was based on living books. The students either read or listened to about forty books read to them during the school year. The theme for year six was studying the "10/40 Window," which is the place on the globe where the major world religions began and where the greatest number of unreached people groups reside. I was used to traditional academic information for social studies, like teaching my kids about American history with Abraham Lincoln and George Washington and so on. But, in the Sonlight curriculum, we would be learning about Hinduism and Taoism and world religions with which I was unfamiliar.

That year was my first experience of being aware of God's intervention. Night after night, I would receive His God Taps. He would wake me up, prompting me to get up and go into the living room to pray. It reminded me of the Bible story about Samuel. Night after night, I would spend time praying, asking God what He wanted from me. The only thing that I could conclude was that it had something to do with my children and the curriculum that we were supposed to use for the next academic year.

After several nights, maybe even several weeks, I got up the nerve to tell my husband what I was experiencing. He asked me several questions about the research that I had done. He asked me if the curriculum was refundable. I said yes within a certain time. I was very surprised when he suggested that we purchase both curriculums. He said that once I had the materials in my hand, I would know which one to use. So, I ordered both curriculums on the same day. I ordered the Liberty Press textbook curriculum that was the result of their academic testing, and I ordered the Sonlight curriculum, which featured the "10/40 Window." The Sonlight curriculum arrived in about ten days, and the Liberty Press curriculum arrived two months later. We jumped right in and started using the Sonlight curriculum, and within days I knew that it was what the Lord was pressing me to use. We really liked the Sonlight curriculum; it was rich.

We got into a rhythm of reading out of a book called *100 Gateway Cities*. Every day, we would read the recommended reading for a capital city in one of the countries in the 10/40 Window and the specific prayer requests for that country. We would find the city on the world map, push a pin in the city, and get on our knees and pray for the requests for that country. We did this every day for months. Then one day in February, as we repeated our routine, we were directed to pray for Bandar Seri Begawan, the capital city of Brunei, which is located on the island of Borneo. Borneo is the third largest island in the world, divided mainly between Malaysia and Indonesia; Brunei is a Sultanate on the northwestern side of the island tucked in between the East Malaysian states of Sabah and Sarawak. I didn't even know how to pronounce the word *Brunei* much less the name of capital city. As we prayed for this country,

God's Spirit came upon me, and His spirit impressed upon me that He was sending me, or us, to Brunei. I had never experienced anything like that before, and I immediately went into skeptic mode, thinking, "Well, maybe I just had too much pizza too late last night. Maybe I am just hallucinating."

But after that encounter with God, it was intriguing to me how I frequently bumped into more things about Brunei, which was a country I had never heard of before and knew nothing about. Suddenly, it was in the news. Suddenly, it was on the front page of *Life Magazine*. One Sunday we visited a homeschool community church we had never visited before. During their meet and greet time during the worship service, the people in front of us stood up and turned around and introduced themselves. I was facing the husband, and I asked him, "What do you do for a living?" He said, "I make custom staircases." And then he just blurted out, "I'm currently making a custom staircase for the Sultan of Brunei." I remember thinking, "What is the deal with all this Brunei stuff?" The rest of the school year was unremarkable. But we loved the curriculum so much that we decided to use Sonlight curriculum the next year.

Well, the next year, Sonlight guided the kids into writing a special report. It was a report that they would guide the kids through from the beginning to the end of the academic school year. Toward the beginning of the year, they were to choose a country within the 10/40 Window as the subject of their report. My daughter chose Saudi Arabia, and my son surprised me when he chose Brunei. They were instructed to contact missionary organizations to get information about these countries and their ministry needs; my son sent letters, asking for information. Around dinnertime one evening, I received a phone call from the head of Malaysian ministries asking me who was inquiring about Brunei, and why did we want to know. That man's name was Brian. I explained to Brian that my son was doing a report and that he had written the inquiry. I found out that Brian and his family did not live that far from us, just off the freeway in Temple City. Our family was always a home of hospitality, and this time was no different. So, I invited Brian and his wife Esther and their son to come for dinner. They accepted.

They were an interesting and unique couple. Esther was Chinese and had been born in Hudson Taylor's bedroom, in China. As I was serving dinner to our family and theirs, I was carrying a hot steaming platter of spaghetti to the table when I asked Brian what he did before he was involved with ministry. He replied that he used to be chef for the Queen of England, or at least he worked as a chef in the huge kitchens in Central London where they prepare banquet spreads for Buckingham Palace! Well with that information, I almost made an about face with my platter of Ragu smothered spaghetti. We laughed about it and still do to this day. We stayed in touch with Brian and Esther, and then months later, Brian challenged us to go on a prayer walk with Esther and him to Brunei. Now I had always been the kind of Christian who appreciated supporting missionaries financially and praying for them, but I never saw myself as a missionary to be sent. This was a surprising proposition. Not only did we not have the money to go, but we had five children, and our youngest was only three years old. We got conflicting input and responses from our Christian friends. Some enthusiastically encouraged us to go, and others were very concerned about our safety. The Lord directed me to write a support letter thinking that would help us decide whether we should go. Within a very short time, that support letter raised over $11,000. That was enough for my husband, our three oldest children, and me to go on the prayer walk to Brunei.

On the same day, I received two telephone calls, both from homeschool families. One family called and said they had been praying about it and if we went to Brunei, they would be willing to take our youngest daughter for the time that we were gone. I had barely hung up the phone from that conversation, when the phone rang again, and we had another Christian homeschool family offer to take our youngest son. In one day, we made all the arrangements for all seven of us. So, we found ourselves flying to Southeast Asia. We flew from LAX to Kuala Lumpur, Malaysia, where Brian and Esther guided us for several days. We stayed in Kuala Lumpur with a view of the Petronas Twin Towers from our hotel room. We went to Singapore and then to Sarawak, East Malaysia, on the island of Borneo. From Miri, we took a ferry across the River Baram and into Brunei. I will remember the family we stayed with before crossing the river until my dying day. The husband was Indian, and the wife was Chinese. They had two small sons. She had a huge servant's heart, and I can still see her doing my laundry and sitting on the floor folding my underwear. Cheli told a story about his salvation that our entire family will never forget. He told us that as a Hindu son, there was a time in his life when he was so despairing that he was standing either at a river's edge or on a bridge ready to jump and take his life when Jesus appeared to him and transformed his life.

Because of his conversion to Christianity, he was no longer welcome in his Indian family. His mother was a high priestess in the Hindu temple, and his dad was also a man of Hindu influence. Years later he said one of his siblings, I believe it was his sister, committed suicide. The family allowed him to come back for her funeral. When he arrived at the airport, his brother picked him up and as they were getting ready for bed, he heard some ruckus outside in the courtyard and opened the door to see what was going on. I envisioned the home as he described it as a rectangle with a middle courtyard. At that moment his mother, with inches between her feet and the ground, flew into his face and in a demonic voice said to him, "What are you doing here, child of the King?" His mother was demon-possessed, and the demon validated his salvation!

Now in Brunei, we were intentional about walking the streets and praying. We did not know when we went to Brunei what the Lord would have us do there. My husband was considering taking a job and living there as an expatriate. But because of his age, he was too old to do that. I, on the other hand, as a health-care practitioner, was in demand. Brian introduced me to a woman named Andrea. She and I sat for hours talking about health care, homeschooling, and Christianity. She was involved in the underground Christian church in Brunei, which is a strict Muslim nation. Andrea and I developed a code, so we could communicate if there were ever any problems or dangers. We talked in medical language code. Medical procedures did not mean a medical procedure; it meant something else. Andrea and I were sisters in the Lord the minute we met each other. She was a Chinese woman married to a native Bruneian. I was to go home and collect and send her homeschool curriculum catalogs hidden in medical magazines. Brunei likes to think of itself as having freedom of religion. Therefore, they have a few registered churches that people are allowed to attend. As a family we attended an Anglican church, together with Brian, Esther, and Andrea.

If I remember correctly, we returned home from that trip and that prayer walk in September 1999. Our children had many experiences that I am sure contributed to molding and shaping them into the people that they are today. They were surely influenced by what they heard from the people, what they saw, what they ate, and what they smelled. It was a life-influencing trip. The idea of going there to work and live was complicated. Because it was a Muslim country, the husband, had to be employed. If I had worked there as a health-care practitioner, I would not have been allowed to bring my family because I am female. So, to go there and work and live never came to fruition. So, my question was, "Why did God send us there? What was the purpose? Was it just for my children to have this experience, or was there more?" We prayed fervently in many areas of Brunei from around the gold-domed mosque to the river villages.

In January 2000, we were informed that Andrea had been arrested. She had been ripped out of her bed in her family home at ten o'clock at night and incarcerated. No one could tell me where she was or how she was doing. I had felt a bond with this woman, and I became her prayer advocate. We formed an advocacy team for Brunei; families even joined the team from other states. We met at our home in Fallbrook and prayed regularly for Brunei, for the Sultan, and for any other Brunei prayer requests that we were guided to pray for. During that time, I continued to ask about Andrea, but no one was able to give me any information.

As our children continued being homeschooled, they got involved in many activities. Our two oldest sons were actively involved in Civil Air Patrol. Our oldest son was on the Color Guard team, and they competed and made it to a national competition. About the time of this national competition, Brian once again invited us and challenged us to go back to Southeast Asia—this time for a missionary conference. Missionaries from across Southeast Asia would be gathering at one location under the guise of being travel agents. With the busyness of our family, it seemed nearly impossible for us to consider or commit to doing something like that, because of the distance and the expense. But . . . God kept pressing me. Even after we had decided not to go, the nudge or "God Tap" did not go away. I told my husband that God was still pressing us to go. That was 2003. We went to Ohio as a family for my son's Color Guard competition.

When we returned from the competition, one of our Brunei Advocacy team families from Michigan called us. The wife said, "I know that you aren't planning to go to the conference in Southeast Asia. I know that you have already decided not to go, but I just felt like I needed to call and inform you that as of today—today only, on the heels of the SARS epidemic, Singapore Airlines is offering round-trip airfare from Los Angeles International airport to Singapore for $350. When I informed my husband of that information, he surprised me by saying, "Buy seven tickets." I called Singapore Airlines, but the telephone lines were busy for hours. I asked some prayer partners to pray, asking for the phone lines to open for us. Later that evening, I got through and when I asked the ticket agent for seven tickets round-trip from LAX to Singapore, she laughed out loud and said there was no flight that still had that many tickets at that price. I asked her if she would please double-check; she kind of sighed, and I could hear her acrylic nails clicking on the keyboard. Then she exclaimed, "Oh my gosh! Oh my gosh!" And I asked, "What?" And she said, "I just found you seven tickets from LAX to Singapore!" So, that time all seven of us journeyed from the United States to Southeast Asia.

The missionary conference was held north of Singapore in a place called Port Dickson, which is south of Kuala Lumpur. We attended the conference, and it was a very rich time of Christian fellowship. Again, my children met people, saw things, and heard things that contributed to who they are today. On the last day when we were getting ready to wrap up the conference, we had a celebratory ice cream social. Even though we had flown into Singapore, we decided to fly out of Kuala Lumpur because the two younger children had not been with us on the first trip and seen the city. At the ice cream social, a man approached me and asked if I was Victorya. He said that someone wanted to talk to me on the phone. I was hesitant, not exactly sure who would even know I was there. I took the phone and was very surprised to hear Andrea's voice on the other end. She reiterated to me that she remembered every word of our last conversation almost four years prior. I asked her where she was and if she was all right. She spoke with a very flat affect and cautious voice.

She said this was the first time she had been allowed out of Brunei since her incarceration; she said that she was at the University in Kuala Lumpur to take some health-care courses. I informed her that we would be traveling to Kuala Lumpur the next day and asked if I could see her and spend some time together. She was very fearful and very hesitant. I told her I would call her when we got to the hotel, and I would scope out the situation to see where we were staying and what the situation was like. It turned out that we were staying in a very nice hotel and because we were Americans, the hotel had us stay in a room on a secure floor—unless you had a key card to that floor, the elevator passed by that floor. When I informed Andrea of that, she hesitantly said that she would be willing to come to the hotel by taxi. So, I arranged for the concierge to send a taxi to pick her up at the University. I gave her the taxi number and license plate so she would feel confident that the right car was picking her up. When she arrived, she was very timid and fearful and went over to the windows in our room and closed the drapes. Even though we were on the twenty-something floor, she still didn't want anyone to see her in the room. We talked for hours. She shared that she had been incarcerated and that she had been abused. This was the first time that she had been able to talk with anyone about what had happened to her.

By then, it was dinnertime. I suggested that my husband take our children downstairs to the hotel restaurant for dinner, and Andrea and I called for room service. When room service was delivered, Andrea hid in the bathroom so that the server would not know that she was there. I felt sorry for her; her experience had left her very fearful. When my children were out of the room, Andrea was able to share with me even more details about her incarceration and her torture and her abuse. I was stunned. And I was so sad for what she had gone through. This beautiful Christian sister had been so ill-treated. We said our goodbyes, and I sent her back to her college dorm via a hotel taxi. I did not expect to see her again.

I was surprised when the phone rang the next morning, and Andrea told me that the University had canceled classes that day and that she was free to come back. We were going to show our children around Kuala Lumpur before we boarded a plane to return to the United States. But yes, I wanted to see Andrea for one last time. So my husband took the kids downstairs for a meal and I sent a taxi to pick her up from the University, and she came back to our hotel room.

Before she got there that morning, I collected all the leftover Malaysian money, Ringgits, from everyone and put it in a hotel envelope without tabulating how much it was worth. After spending the allotted time with Andrea, it was time for us to part once again. I gave her the envelope and told her to hide it and put it away in case of an emergency, and then I asked her if I could give her a hug, goodbye. I told her that in the United States when we say goodbye to family or friends, we hug, and she acknowledged that she was OK if I did that. So, I reached over and put my arms around her to give her a hug, but unlike hugs here in the United States where you hug and let go, she did not let go. She held onto me, and we both began to sob.

At that moment, I realized that all those years before when God woke me up and directed me which curriculum to use that it was for that moment—for this precious Christian sister who had been kidnapped, incarcerated, tortured and had no one that she could share the trauma with. There we were—seven Americans free to come and go, but God had orchestrated for us to be there for her as she recovered from the ordeal that she had experienced. I was safe to talk to. I was safe to share with. God sent us there specifically as an answer to Andrea's prayers. Not once, but twice.

As we were packing our luggage getting ready to go to the airport to fly home, I got one final phone call from Andrea on the hotel room phone. She told me that after she left, she had gotten a call from her husband in Brunei and that they were at risk of losing their home unless they came up with a specific payment or fine that was being imposed on them. I told Andrea, "Open the envelope." When she did, she told me that it was the amount that they needed to cover the fine and to keep their home.

BRUNEI

For safety reasons, Andrea and I do not keep in touch. I still pray for her and consider her my forever sister. We are sisters bonded forever for eternity.

ROSIE

I call this the God Story about writing the God Storys. Over the past five years, some of my prayer partners have strongly suggested that I write out my God Storys and for whatever reason, I have always been very resistant to do that. I am a very private person, and sharing my God Storys just didn't feel right to me. I love proclaiming what God has done through the people He has brought into my life, but making the stories public was out of my comfort zone. Then in January 2019, I felt God directing me to do two things.

For the first time ever in the past five years, I felt God nudging me to write out my God Storys. I had no plan; I had no real thought of how that would come about, but it was the first time, I was no longer resistant, for I knew that was what I was being directed to do. Second, I felt that I needed to be intentional about getting to know my cousin Rosie. Now Rosie is the youngest daughter of my aunt and uncle, my mother's sister, the fifth of six children. My aunt and uncle had lived in Santa Cruz, California, my whole entire life, but they passed away some years ago. With their passing, Rosie and I talked about spending some time together and getting to know each other better. She is the youngest daughter in her family, and I am the oldest daughter in mine.

There is an eight-year age difference between us, which in the past prevented us from building a long-distance relationship. I contacted Rosie in either January or February telling her that I would like to schedule a time to visit her in Santa Cruz. I remember that her parents had lived in a very beautiful area of Santa Cruz with lush gardens. So I suggested going to visit her, and we began to explore the possibilities.

"Rosie," I said, "Not only would I like to come and visit you, spend some time with you, and get to know you better, but I also would like to take some time to write."

"Oh, what are you going to write about?" she asked.

I said, "Well, I would like to write my God storys."

Now as cousins, we didn't know each other very well, so she asked, "Oh, are you a spiritual person?"

"Well, yes, but I like to consider myself more relational."

"Well, if you are going to come to Santa Cruz to visit me and you are planning to write while you are here, then you should visit me in my other home instead of coming to Santa Cruz. I live part of the time in Twain Harte, which is near Yosemite, in the Sierra Nevada Mountains."

"Well, I don't care where I visit you at," I responded. "I just want to spend some time with you. If I am going to be in the Sierra Nevada Mountains, I would prefer it would be at a time that there isn't any snow. I really don't care to drive in the snow."

Rosie mentioned that she cleans houses to earn a living and that one of her clients lives on seven acres of forest and that he has a main house and a guesthouse. She offered to ask him if he would be willing to rent the guesthouse to me at a discount.

My finances were very strapped and tight ever since our divorce, and so I was thankful for her intercession and her willingness to ask the owner if I could rent his guesthouse at an affordable price. In early March, when she was in Twain Harte, she texted me that the owner,

John, would like to talk to me, and she sent me his phone number. So that evening I texted John and asked if that was a convenient time to talk. So, we talked on the phone, and he introduced himself saying that he had been widowed about a year ago since his wife passed away from cancer.

John was living on seven acres of forest and had a guesthouse that he rented out through Airbnb. He asked me what I was planning to write about, and I told him my God storys. He told me that he was a Lutheran pastor and that if I was coming to visit him to use his guesthouse, he would charge me nothing. I was happily surprised by his generosity, and I knew immediately that this was God's way of encouraging me to continue moving forward with His nudge to write. Without the discount or without John's generosity, it would have been very difficult for me to go and write for an extended time. John said, "Just tell me the dates, and I will block them for you." So he blocked the dates, and I planned to arrive on May 16th and leave on May 29th. So, I had a gift from John and from the Lord of thirteen days in a beautiful guesthouse on seven acres of forest in the Sierra Nevada Mountains.

When I left for Twain Harte, we had days of rain with a forecast of more rain. Now I intensely dislike driving in the rain, but I was really excited about getting to my destination, so I asked my prayer partners to support me in prayer as I drove what was going to be seven hours in the rain from Carlsbad through Los Angeles to Twain Harte, which is near Yosemite. Driving in the rain is messy and inconvenient, and there are greater chances of more traffic and accidents. Over the years, I had developed a fear of driving in the rain; it had become kind of a white-knuckle experience, so I was not enthusiastic about driving a projected seven hours in the downpour.

Jerry, my biblical counselor, brother in the Lord, and friend sent me a text suggesting that I listen to a song called "No Longer

Slaves" while I drive. I arrived safely in Twain Harte around dinnertime an hour and a half later than my projected ETA, but I was safe and sound. The next day I sent this email: "Hello, Jerry. I am finally settled into my beautiful little guesthouse. I really like the song that you recommended, wonderful lyrics."

I had listened to "No Longer Slaves" while driving in the rain. Although I had always disliked driving in the rain, I am no longer a slave to fear; I am a child of God, and the song really helped and empowered me. I had to laugh. As I drove, I prayed and asked God to have the rain cease or at least become just mist. Instead, he transformed my attitude about the rain. I was able to see the drive as symbolic of life—my life, all of life—and of what I was directed to write about here. As I drove those eight hours, I passed through torrential storms as well as blue skies and sunlit clouds. I experienced the greatest variety of weather I have ever driven in.

I spent Friday, Saturday, Sunday, and Monday with Rosie. We spent hours hiking and looking at God's majestic creation, looking at wildflowers along the trails, reminiscing about our mothers and their love for gardening and flowers, and recalling how they would have liked the blue bonnets that grew by the side of the trail. We got to know each other better and laughed a lot as we bumped into our similarities often. Sometimes, we would say the same thing at the same time, and then we would be playful and tease that we were twins, though we look nothing alike. Rosie takes after the German side of our family, and I take after the Italian side of mine, but we would hoot it up and go cheek-to-cheek and tell friends, "Look, we are twins." It was four fun days. Rosie took good care of me and, as I write this story, I am settled into John's guesthouse on seven acres of forest in the Sierra Nevada Mountains proclaiming what God has done . . . for His glory.

ROSIE

JOI

My husband, Mac, and I were married for about thirty-four years. Twenty of those years were very good, and I used to tell people that my husband was perfect. In those first twenty years, I helped him go back to graduate school, get his master's degree, and go into private practice as a Christian licensed marriage and family therapist in two counties. I don't know exactly what happened after those first twenty years, but I do know that the fourteen years that followed were very difficult for a variety of reasons. In the difficult years, God sent me Joi. He sent "joy" spelled J-O-I in a new friend and J-O-Y as in the fruit of the Holy Spirit.

It was the beginning of the Christmas season, and we were putting up our Christmas tree and lights and decorating the house the day after Thanksgiving like we did almost every year. But because of poor planning or no planning, the mood was getting a little combative, and I developed a very angry disposition when I was asked to go to the local drugstore to purchase more lights for our live Christmas tree. I found myself at the local Rite-Aid store about an hour before closing time. I purchased the items I had been asked to get, brought them back home only to find out that I did not get the string of lights that we needed, and so I had to make another trip, which only enhanced my bad attitude and my anger.

As I shopped in the aisle of Christmas paraphernalia, particularly the stringed lights section, I did not want to see anyone that I knew. I did not want to encounter anyone. So, no surprise as I am on my second trip just minutes before the store closes, I come around a corner, and there is Joi. Joi is a very friendly homeschool mom whom I did not know very well, but she was a part of our local homeschool support group. It wasn't that I didn't want to see Joi; I didn't want to see anyone. So, I gritted my teeth and smiled through my teeth, tried to be friendly even though I didn't feel like it one bit. Joi and I did not talk for very long. We just greeted one another and exchanged a few niceties, and I went on my way not thinking anything of the encounter. The next day, I went to the local post office to get our mail from the PO box and, as I drove up, there was Joi getting out of her car and going into the post office. I was in a better mood that time, so we had a little more of an exchange; then I went to get my mail out of the PO box, and she went to mail the package that was in her hand. A few days later when I got mail at home, there was a package from Joi; I was a little surprised. I opened it and found a music CD of praise and worship songs with a note that just said, "God told me to send this to you."

Well that act of obedience on Joi's part was the beginning of a new friendship and a solid prayer partnership for years afterward. I listened to that praise and worship CD over and over again, and I noticed that the songs were lifting my spirits and transforming my attitude. And then one day as I was driving and listening to the songs, I got what I call a God Tap when I realized that God had intentionally sent that music CD to me through Joi for me to recognize that I needed true joy in my life. Joi and her family moved to Northern California and beyond, so I don't see her as often as I once did. But she and I are faithful prayer warriors for each other, and every time I see her name come up as a text on my phone, I remember that CD, and I remember God's directive for me to have true joy, His joy, the fruit of the Holy Spirit, in my life at all times no matter what the circumstances.

ADAM

At this time, four of our five children had graduated from homeschool high school and were attending college. My youngest daughter was still living at home, and we were homeschooling high school. As part of her homeschool curriculum, I had her attending a weekly women's Bible study at the church with me in Escondido. One day, she had some assignments that she had to do. Our routine was that, after Bible study, she would go upstairs to a room where she would do her schoolwork, and I would bring work to do, and we would wait until youth group that same evening. That was a routine that we were familiar with and implemented on a weekly basis.

That day, the work that she had to do involved some audio that she had to play back, and I felt that I couldn't concentrate on the work I had to do, so I left her in one of the classrooms upstairs, and I relocated to the church library. Although I had volunteered and frequented the library, I had never spent any time in that space. As I was sitting in an overstuffed vintage chair in the library doing my work, I felt God drawing my eyes to a particular place in the library. I squinted trying to figure out the title on the spine of one of the books. What was it on the cover? From where I was sitting, I couldn't read it, but it became evident to me that I was being drawn to that specific book. I got up to get the book and read the title, *The Silence of Adam*. Although I had volunteered in the library many times, I do not recall ever seeing that book before. As I took it off the shelf and started perusing it, I was really surprised at what I was reading.

I read the book from cover to cover that same day; it gave me the information and Christian perspective that I needed to understand what was wrong in my marriage. The basic gist of it recalled Adam and Eve in the garden when Eve was tempted by the serpent to disobey God. The revelation I received from that book, which I hadn't been aware of at the time, was that Adam was actually in the garden with Eve when she was tempted. What was hard for me to comprehend, a very important fact for me, was that Adam did nothing. He did not protect Eve; he did not battle the serpent; he passively allowed that whole fall to occur.[2]

Adam had been commanded by God to be the head of his family, Eve, and to obey God by not eating the fruit from the tree of the knowledge of good and evil. His disobedience and passivity were passed down to all generations since that moment in history. *The Silence of Adam* was instrumental in helping me understand what was terribly wrong in my marriage. I bought extra copies of the book and gave it to my husband. He read it and agreed. However, nothing changed or improved in the role or participation of his leadership. Up until that point, I had not received any real understanding about my marriage and what was wrong from the counseling sessions that we attended.

You might remember that, in the early days of our marriage, I was the one who did not want children. Well over the years, as I homeschooled and as my children developed friendships with other children, not only did I have all my children, but I also had some of their friends as my symbolically "adopted" children. One of those bonus sons, Andrew, married Jeannette and as Mama Wright, I attended their wedding ceremony at a church in Orange

County. Nestled in their wedding ceremony was a brief homily by Pastor Crimson who was performing the ceremony. I was so caught off guard and so unprepared for the message of that homily. Pastor Crimson spoke to the groom about his responsibilities in his marriage, and he summarized in that brief homily the contents of *The Silence of Adam*. I had never heard anyone in the church preach that message before.

A few weeks later I was playing phone tag with a woman from my church. She and I had committed to house a seminary student for a time, and we were going to split the time between us. Rebecca was a very busy woman, and it was hard for us to coordinate our schedules and have a conversation and agree on the shared dates. These were the early days of cell phones, and I did not have hands-free Bluetooth at the time, but I could see on my cell phone that Rebecca was returning my phone call. I didn't want to miss her call, so I pulled over to talk to her and parked for the duration of the call. Rebecca was a friend, a Christian woman, whom I greatly respected, and I didn't want to just jump into discussing the task we had before us, so I intentionally inquired as to her health because I knew she had been having some serious health issues. In the conversation, she told me that she had done a lot of research on her own and had concluded that she had a very rare condition that not too many people understood or treated.

The words that she spoke next would change my life forever. She said that she had taken her research to a doctor in our church, and he concurred with her conclusion. However, he recommended that instead of taking her results to her doctor that she should find out what doctor in the United States understood her condition to treat it effectively. When she spoke those words, the Holy Spirit came upon me with the words, "Go to the person who gets it." And I knew at that moment that I needed to connect with Pastor Crimson who had spoken that homily, who was the only person I had met who understood *The Silence of Adam* and the ramifications and repercussions of that silence in relationships, generation after generation, which had ended up affecting my home, my marriage, and the training of my sons and daughters.

God used a casual planning conversation with Rebecca and a fifteen-minute homily to impact my life and the life of my family. Was this (A) coincidence or (B) God-orchestrated? I pick answer B.

JENNA

It was December 2012, and Christmas was upon us. For weeks with all the busyness of preparation and planning, I was experiencing unusual heart palpitations and discomfort. Our family was planning to go to a cabin in Mammoth, California, between Christmas and New Year's to enjoy some family time in the snow-covered mountains. Just days before Christmas, I had an appointment with my cardiologist, and he detected that I was experiencing dangerous cardiac arrythmias. He asked me to see a specialist, a cardiac electrophysiologist. Instead of finding myself in a mountain cabin in Mammoth after Christmas, I found myself in a hospital in San Bernadino having a catheter ablation for my cardiac arrythmias. My husband and my oldest son took me to the hospital.

I remember that my feelings were hurt as I was being rolled into the procedure room when my husband said that, while I was there, he was planning to go to an air museum to look at airplanes. The procedure was unexpectedly traumatic because I did not have profound anesthesia, so I felt and heard everything. I smelled my own flesh being seared as they cauterized my heart. I heard the attendant say, "Give her some more medication; she is moaning." Someone else said, "The pharmacy is back-ordered; there isn't any more of that." That evening, it was my son who spooned dinner into my mouth, chuckling that this was a foreshadowing of the future. It was weeks before I was allowed to climb stairs or lift heavy objects.

No one had prepared me for what happened next: This procedure unexpectedly catapulted me into a biological depression. I had never experienced anything like it before. I could not stop crying. I emailed the pastor of my church with pleas for help, and he recommended that I see a Christian psychiatrist or therapist. He gave me a referral to Jenna, a Christian marriage and family therapist, who had published several books about Christian living. Jenna recommended that I see a Christian psychiatrist and start medication to help me through the biological depression. I met with the psychiatrist only a few times when I realized that my body's sensitivity to any medication meant that I experienced whatever side effects the medication might have, and I did have unwanted side effects. So I quit taking the medication earlier than anticipated. However, I continued going to therapy sessions with Jenna. She was a very well-educated, intuitive, understanding, and compassionate therapist. She was a good listener and shared her counsel based on the Word of God.

For two or three sessions, my husband was invited to join the sessions so that we could work on our relationship and our marriage, but they were unsuccessful. I continued to work on myself for about two years with Jenna.

In time, I recognized that the heart arrythmias that I experienced were a necessary part of God's design to lead me to Jenna.

FAMILY TSUNAMI

For the last three months of 2013 and the first six months of 2014, I experienced an irreparable emotional hemorrhage. For years my marriage had been punctuated with aloneness, emptiness, emotional abandonment, secrets, dishonesty, wandering eyes, and countless broken promises. For more than a decade, I had begged and pleaded to be known and loved. Sorrowfully, our marriage had been reduced to a state where when, at times, I felt like a surrogate and Clydesdale workhorse in the relationship. We were no longer an "us." I recognized later that, along the way, I had lost myself.

In July 2014, God directed me to communicate with Pastor Crimson. We met for a two-hour session and then met again the same afternoon for additional time. After listening, he counseled me to separate from my husband. That was unexpected counsel, not something I had considered prior to then. I was a Christian wife, and I understood my responsibilities as a Christian in my marriage, despite circumstances. When he directed me to separate *soon*, it was for the sole intent of rebooting and reconciling, not for the purpose of divorcing.

When I met with my Christian counselor, Jenna, and relayed the conversations that I had with the Pastor Crimson, she concurred with his recommendation. Professionally, she was limited in what she could counsel me to do, but that she was in agreement with Pastor Crimson's directive. At this juncture, I was like a deer in the headlights, just processing this advice, this thought. How would I do this? When would I do this? How could I afford to do this? Where would I go? Then I reached out to my friends and prayer partners: Each one with whom I shared this information concurred that this was a necessary step in healing my marriage.

I had nowhere to go. My youngest daughter had recently graduated from homeschool high school and was getting ready to start her freshman year at Biola University. I had anticipated this being a special time when we would prepare her for this transition. However if I was going to leave and separate even though there was no good time to do this, God directed me to leave two weeks before school started so my daughter would have the support of family and her church community and friends rather than having the tsunami hit while she was a freshman in college. Pastor Crimson told me not to worry about the kids. He told me to write an email to all of them as a group, informing them of my intention to separate from their father; I was to keep the email very brief and simple. I remember thinking that it didn't feel right to me. I had a very special relationship with all my kids; an email felt so impersonal, but since I knew that God was directing me in all this, I accepted that he was being God-directed, so I followed his advice.

God provided for me in a variety of ways the day I separated. Bob at Bald Eagle Movers along with my three friends—Vicki, Katherine, and Sharon—helped me to pack up half of my household to move. I had met a real estate agent named John who felt sorry for me and made it his mission to find me a place to live, and he was instrumental in finding a two-bedroom, two bath condo for me in Bonsall. In the evening of the day that I left, my husband called me; he sounded like he had been crying, and he told me that he would do anything to win me back. I asked that we begin counseling again; we had been through multiple counselors over the years, and my request was that we go to a counselor who did not know either of us. Pastor Crimson recommended a counselor in Orange County; this person was a trained professional who had not met either of us and did not know my counselor husband. Countless times over the years of our marriage, my husband would say or promise to do something, but then he would never follow through. This was no different than the other times.

When we walked into our therapist's office for the first time after the separation, Mac walked up to the therapist, extended his hand to shake hands and said, "Hello, I am Mac. I am Vickie's fourth husband." That was my early, painful cue that reconciliation was unlikely, if not hopeless. There was no, "I love you" or repentance; there was no communication of wanting to heal or fix our marriage. There was only anger, hostility, and wounded pride. To make things worse, Mac informed me that he would never do anything ever to pursue me.

The weeks, months, and even years that followed this tsunami were very difficult. However, this was a time of growing in my relationship with God. He, God, was my true husband. He continued to direct me every step of the way. I have come to recognize God's direction in my life. He has different ways of getting my attention and guiding me, but this was the first time, He communicated in what I call "the threes." I now have an agreement with God. Whenever he communicates to me in threes, I pay attention. This time it was first, Pastor Crimson; second, Jenna; and third, close personal friends. Without knowing each other and without talking to each other, they all gave the same counsel, the same directions. God got my attention, and I was compelled to take action.

WAKE UP

In February 2015, I was sound asleep one night when the Lord woke me up with one of His God Taps or inaudible God Whispers. These God Taps are always very different from other awakenings. They are different from the awakenings from an interruption of noise in the night or the night sweats of hormone imbalance or three in the morning wakefulness with a mind full of thoughts. They are always similar in that I can sense God's presence and that He is directing me in some way. These God Taps remind me of the Scripture when God called the boy Samuel four times. Samuel finally responded, *"Speak. I'm your servant, ready to listen"* (1 Samuel 3:10 MSG). That morning, God directed me to check out my Verizon cell phone bill. Now that was an odd, random suggestion; I kept questioning whether I was hearing Him correctly, but the direction was very specific and unrelenting. I had overseen all the administrative aspects of our home, not because I wanted to but because, through Mac's abdication, I had to. Mac's abdication in our marriage began noticeably in 2002.

The Verizon telephone bill was available online, and I had easy access to it. I did not know why God was directing me to look at the Verizon bill. I did not know what I was looking for, but in the wee hours of the morning or the middle of the night, I got up, bleary-eyed; I obediently started perusing the Verizon cell phone bill. As I looked through several months of billing, I recognized that a certain phone number appeared repeatedly; it was a number that my husband had called on a regular basis for months. I had no idea whose number it was; I didn't know whether it was a counselee or a business associate, but it was a very repetitive number on the bill.

He began calling this number regularly twenty-one days after we separated. I plugged the number into Google and couldn't believe my eyes when the number came up for Judy.

So, twenty-one days after we separated, instead of putting forth an effort to restore our marriage or reconcile, he initiated a relationship with Judy. I knew Judy. I did not like Judy. Judy had been married to Jim. My husband had flown in the Navy with Jim as part of a Navy helicopter search and rescue squadron. The squadron couples had been friends and buddies for many years. In our first year of marriage, Judy had written a letter to my husband that was entirely inappropriate, and I was upset by the letter. At that juncture my husband assured me that it would never happen again, but I was never comfortable around Judy at the squadron reunions. There are very few people in my life that I can say I don't like, but Judy has always been one of them. I never trusted her. For months, the Verizon bill showed a combination of phone calls and texts, hundreds of them every month.

So, my husband had chosen to initiate a relationship with Judy instead of keeping his promise to do whatever it took to win me back. After a while, I realized I was dealing with emotional abandonment and infidelity, and I knew that it was time to terminate the marriage and convert the legal separation to a divorce. If God had not awakened me at two in the morning and directed me to check the Verizon bill, I don't know how much time would have passed before I understood the real, hopeless condition of our marriage.

The months and years that followed this tsunami affected my relationships with all my adult children. But God has been gracious to make new my relationships with them. I did not anticipate or expect that wake-up nudge from the Lord that morning in February, but it was a turning point in my future and the future of my entire family.

DAWN

For three years after our separation, communication and interaction with my youngest daughter was minimal, almost nonexistent. That was a very emotionally difficult time for me as I saw my youngest child and her college experience as something with which I had hoped to be integrally involved. I wanted to know what she was learning. I wanted to know about her instructors. I wanted to know about her new friends and her activities, but I was not included in any of that. She had the advantage of starting college with a semester of college credits that were completed while she was still in high school.

The original plan was for her to spend less on college tuition and to graduate at least a semester, if not a year earlier; but for the first semester of her sophomore year, as a history major, she decided to take a family genealogy-history trip all around the United States doing a personal research project on family genealogy. One of her instructors was giving her college credit for this project. She made her plans with one-way airline tickets to go visit family members and family friends all over the United States for that full semester. It was my understanding that it was recommended that she visit some of our homeschool friends, particularly one in Colorado, whose name was Dawn.

I originally knew Dawn in my early homeschool years because we lived in the same town, the same community, and she had been homeschooling longer than I had, so she showed me the ropes so to speak. Her kids were older than mine, so she had a head start. We had been good friends and prayer partners, and we went through some difficult times together when each of us experienced the trauma, sadness, and difficulty of miscarriage. Dawn and her husband Ben and their family moved from Fallbrook to Washington State, from Washington State to North Carolina, and from North Carolina to Colorado. We were both busy moms homeschooling large families, and even though we still had a strong affection for each other, we didn't have a lot of communication during those next few years because of the busyness of our lifestyles. However, we always stayed in touch.

When I heard that my daughter was going to visit my friend Dawn, I realized that it would be unfair for Dawn to hear the news of our separation and pending divorce from my daughter instead of hearing it from me. So, I was intentional about trying to get in touch with Dawn not only to catch up with her as a dear friend but also to get her up to speed as to what was going on in our family and in our home. We played phone tag for weeks.

We finally connected the day before my daughter was supposed to arrive. The conversation went something like this.

"Sorry it has been so long since we have talked. So much has happened. I just wanted to get you up to speed and, with my daughter coming tomorrow, I wanted you to hear it from me instead of from her, that Mac and I are in the process of getting a divorce."

Dawn's response was of shock and sadness, "Oh, my gosh," she said. "I had no idea. I am so sorry, but you should know that Ben and I separated, and a divorce is likely on the horizon."

I couldn't believe my ears. It was already hard enough for me to go through the experience but for a friend to also be going through it was terrible.

Dawn then started telling me about a condition, "Intimacy Anorexia," that a therapist had told her that her husband Ben had. She sent me a book and DVDs, explaining this condition. I had never heard of it before, but I watched the DVD. It presented several bullet points describing this condition; it said something like this: "If someone has three to five of these characteristics, then it is likely that they have intimacy anorexia." After watching the DVD and reading the book, I realized that my husband, or soon to be ex-husband, had all the characteristics listed. The information about the condition helped me to understand and process what I was dealing with in my marriage. It finally started to make sense—very sad sense. Dawn and I talk and pray for each other frequently.

We soon realized that we had been living parallel lives ever since she and her husband moved from Fallbrook and were on their journey of moving to different states. Even miles apart, we continued to live parallel lives not realizing that we would have this reencounter with one another at this very difficult time of separation and divorce. We would pray for one another; no one else really understood what we were going through. When things made no sense or did not seem fair, we had each other. Dawn was a gift from God to me at a very crucial and difficult time in my life. She remains my prayer partner, my sister in the Lord, my dearest friend. Over the past decade, we have come to describe ourselves as Doppelgänger friends . . . except for the vast difference in our height, we are replicas of each other.

God provided and orchestrated for me to go to Colorado and spend time with Dawn face-to-face twice over the last decade. Our friendship is a real-life manifestation of Galatians 6:2: *"Carry each other's burdens, and in this way you will fulfil the law of Christ."*

In time, with forgiveness and answered prayer, my relationship with my youngest daughter is restored, renewed, and a beautiful gift.

GOD STORYS

MADISON

In my experience, it has been more difficult to make new friends in my senior years than it was in earlier years when I was interacting with different groups of people related to our kids, church, and otherwise. It is also more difficult to make new friends when you are going through a difficult season of life of trials and suffering. God knows what we need. God knew what I needed, so he brought me Madison. When I separated from my husband, I needed to separate my finances; therefore, I opened a bank account at a new bank. I didn't do much research on the bank I chose. It was more a geographical decision of convenience than of researching the bank itself. When I opened the new bank account, I don't think that the bank offered online banking. In the past, when I handled the administrative aspects in of our home, I utilized online banking.

A few years after I opened this account, the bank began offering online banking. The setup and implementation of the online banking was a little bumpy. After a while, the bank went through a computer conversion, and that affected its online banking in a significant way; I began having a terrible time getting my bank account to work accurately and smoothly. Whenever I went into the branch with my complaints and challenges, they would tell me to reregister, and so I did. But even after I reregistered, I could not get my online banking to work. Days and weeks went by, and I got more and more frustrated trying to bank without it working properly. Finally, one day the manager at my branch recommended that I call the online banking department and work with them rather than going through the branch. The following Monday, I called the online banking department and was put in contact with a woman named Madison. Now Madison had only been working there for a week or so, and she mentioned that the software conversion had caused a lot of issues for customers.

She examined my account and reported that it was a tangled mess. Each time I reregistered as instructed by the branch, it had further tangled my account. She said that she was going to help me, but that it would take some time. Every day for a week, I would get a call from Madison either asking questions or reporting her progress at untangling my mess. By Friday, I learned to recognize her number when she called. I was in a happy silly mood when I saw her number come across my screen on a Friday afternoon. So, when I answered her call, instead of the typical greeting of hello, I said, "When are we going out to lunch?" Now, of course, I was just kidding. I had no idea where Madison worked or lived. She could have been in India for all I knew as a virtual assistant. But her next words really caught me off guard. She said, "It's funny you would say that because I was going to ask you if ever get to Escondido?" Now, Escondido is the next good-sized city south of Fallbrook in San Diego County. I said to her, "Well, it is funny you should ask. I am leaving here any minute after I hang up talking to you to go to Escondido to complete my final discipleship session with my pastor's wife." She and her husband were getting ready to move from Escondido to South Carolina so that he could teach in a seminary. We were in the process of wrapping up and completing the discipleship that we had enjoyed together, and this was going to be our last day together.

MADISON

Madison asked me if I would like to meet her that evening in Escondido for a drink. I was so caught off guard that my mind was racing with thoughts of, "Who is this person, and why is she asking me this?" I was uncomfortable with the proposition. I didn't answer her right away, but told her I would think about it and get back to her. Driving to Escondido to meet with my pastor's wife, my friend Caroline and I prayed about it. I felt the Lord directing me to say yes and to meet with Madison. And so despite my discomfort and out of obedience, I told Madison, yes, I would meet her for a drink. She picked a place that was right down the street from the church where I was meeting with Caroline, and so that was unusually convenient. After my Bible study and discipleship time, I simply drove down the same street to the designated restaurant.

Now this was a very upscale restaurant above a car dealership. That alone was unusual. I arrived at the restaurant, found a place to sit not knowing what Madison even looked like. I ordered a glass of wine and waited, and then Madison approached, asking if I was Victorya. We began a conversation, and we talked for hours. She told me that she lived in the mountain community of Ramona and that she drove to Escondido to work every day. She said that she was a Christian but that she did not attend a church. She was grieving the loss of her husband who had recently died in his sleep of a brain bleed. She had awakened one morning and found him dead lying next to her. She said she was attracted to me because of my email address, 7savedbygrace.com. She gathered from my email address that I was a Christian. She had been praying and asking God to bring her a female friend who was a Christian to come alongside her. That was the motivation for her invitation that day.

We have since talked and met a few times. When she was on vacation, she came to Carlsbad, and we had a nice dinner together.

We really enjoyed getting to know each other and developing a new friendship. So even in these senior years, God has been faithful to bring new friends to come alongside us, to lift us up, to bear each another's burdens. When I was frustrated with my matted and messy online banking account, I saw it as an inconvenience and annoyance, not as a gift. I had no idea that God would use that inconvenience to gift me with a new Christian friend.

TONYA

After I discovered that my husband was pursuing a relationship with Judy instead of pursuing a relationship with me, God directed me to write a letter to Judy. I had no interest in writing a letter to Judy. I didn't even know what to say or where to begin, but as God has done many times over the years, when He wants me to write a letter and He wants His words to be my words and my words to be His words, He writes the letter for me, usually in my head; all I have to do is have Him use my fingers on the keyboard to write His letter out. So, even in my resistant state, I obeyed His direction and wrote the letter as He wrote the words for me. I sent the letter to Judy certified, and I received no response. I had not expected any response, so that did not surprise me, but it left me baffled as to why God would have me write it in the first place.

The gist of the letter was asking Judy to leave my husband alone. Sometime later, weeks later to my recollection, God directed me to send copies of that letter with a cover letter to three or four other people. Two of the people were the pastors of the church that I had been attending before the family tsunami hit. One certified letter was addressed to my senior pastor, and the other one was addressed to our associate pastor. Both cover letters were identical except for name changes. For five years prior to our separation, I had met with them and asked both pastors multiple times to help us with our marriage and to intercede in our difficulties. There was very little or no response to my pleas. As a result, Pastor Crimson and Jenna and our new counselor strongly recommended that I stop attending that church. However, I was a member of that church, and I take membership very seriously. At God's direction, I felt led to make one last attempt by sending the Judy letter along with a cover letter asking my previous pastors to intercede in this immoral and destructive situation. Their lack of response once again was disappointing, yet not unexpected.

This was a very sensitive and personal letter. After investigating the tracking of the certified letters, I learned after several weeks that only three of the five letters made it to their destinations. I became concerned that my letters were just sitting somewhere on a desk in a post office or in a city for which they were never intended. I monitored those letters for weeks, even months and was never able to find where they ended up. I went online to the USPS website and filed a claim to look for the lost certified letters. I was living in Bonsall at the time, so I was surprised when I received a phone call one day from the postal supervisor of Customer Service in Carlsbad. Her name was Tonya. I was surprised to be contacted by the Carlsbad office because the letters were mailed from the Fallbrook post office. Tonya left a voicemail for me, telling me that she had been assigned to find the lost letters but that she needed some additional information from me. She left a phone number and asked me to call her.

At the time, I was living in Carlsbad, and I was in the habit of swimming almost every day. I received Tonya's voice message while I was at the community pool. On the way home from the pool, I tried calling her number and the call either would not go through, or the phone just rang. Even though I had just come out of the pool and was still somewhat wet from swimming, I chose to go to the post office in my wet bathing suit and cover-up. When I got to the post office, I asked to speak with Tonya. She came out and was very professional; she was helpful, friendly, and sympathetic. I explained about my attempt to call the number that she gave me. I called it again while I was standing there at the counter, and wouldn't you know, I had egg on my face because the number rang through while I was standing there. For some reason, it seemed that I needed to go physically to the post office rather than respond via telephone call. Tonya told me what information she needed; however, I did not have that information with me, so I had to go home, look up the information, and get it back to her. Since I had difficulty reaching her on the original phone number she had given me, she gave me her personal cell phone and suggested that I call or text the information to her on that number. I was a little surprised at her willingness to do that, but I was happy about it, hoping that I would be able to retrieve my letters.

As I was leaving the post office still with wet hair and wet suit underneath my coverup, Tonya asked, "Do you like wine? I was quite taken back by the question, so I kind of sputtered an answer back at her, "Well, uh, yes . . . why do you ask?" She told me that she was a pretty good judge of character and that she thought that she and I would enjoy being friends. Tonya and I later enjoyed each other's company over a glass of wine and cheese and crackers. And we have enjoyed sharing our life experiences as Christian women. We plan to maintain this friendship for all eternity. I went from being frustrated and even apprehensive to being thankful for a new friend. Again, in this senior season of life when friendships are harder to come by, God has given me Tonya.

SNAKES

I was happy and appreciative to be in my condo in Bonsall. For a few months before my one-year lease was up, God began communicating to me that I was going to move. I did not know when, and I did not know where, but I did know that I was going to move. When my lease came up for renewal, my landlady asked me to sign a new one-year lease; I informed her that I would be moving but that I didn't know where or when. I asked her if I could stay on a month-to-month basis instead of signing another lease. She told me that she did not do month-to-month and that it was customary for her to do a lease. I asked if she would make an exception. She told me she liked me as a tenant and that she would in this one circumstance make an exception and, therefore, I went from a lease to a month-to-month tenant.

In the next six months, there was an instance that caused me to wake very early in the morning. I am not a super early riser; I can either be a morning person or a night person depending on the day, the time, and the circumstances. But I had a lot to do that day, so I woke up unusually early—around five in the morning; it was still dark outside. Instead of going back to sleep I talked myself into getting up and starting on my day to get a lot accomplished. It was dark, and it was chilly. I put on my robe and slippers and went from my bedroom into the living room. I turned on the light and as I did, I perceived some peripheral movement. As I turned my head, there in my living room, up against my sliding glass door, was a coiled adult snake. It was looking at me eyeball to eyeball and I was terrified. I hate snakes!

I could not tell what kind of snake it was. It had the coloring of a rattlesnake, but because it was coiled, I couldn't see its tail, and it was not rattling . . . yet. My mind raced. What was I going to do? What was it doing here? How did it get in? How long has it been there? And then above my head, I heard movement and a toilet flush, and I knew my neighbor on the second floor was awake. Without losing eye contact with the snake, I reached for my phone and called Kendall. I said "Kendall, I need your help. I have a snake in my living room." He said, " I am not dressed." I said, "I will wait." In the meantime, I think the snake started getting used to me and it started to uncoil and then I really panicked because I was thinking what if it gets underneath my bed in my bedroom, what if it gets underneath my couch, or what if it gets under my refrigerator? Keeping eye contact with the snake, I slowly moved to the left and closed my bedroom door; I was able to throw a jacket in front of the crack underneath the door to discourage the snake from going underneath the crack in the door. Then again, the snake started to uncoil when I took a jacket off the back of a chair and like a toreador, I took the jacket to the snake, and it recoiled.

After what seemed like a hundred years, Kendall showed up with the longest barbecue tongs I have ever seen, and he was able to grab the snake behind its head and take it away. I did not want to know what he did with it. It was a very large adult king snake, which I am told is harmless but having had that snake coiled and looking at me first thing in the morning was both terrifying and exhausting. I spent the rest of the day recovering from the trauma of that morning.

SNAKES

About a week later, I came home from running an errand to the shock of having a large puddle of fresh red blood in front of my doorway. It looked as if someone had been stabbed. Now where I lived in Bonsall was not beautiful, but it was safe. So I was really baffled as to what had happened and who was injured and how it happened. I inquired of all my neighbors, and no one knew what the blood was from. That evening my neighbors to the east of me toward the valley came home, and I inquired of them, and the husband said to me, "Go look in the back of my truck."

When I looked in the back of his pickup truck, I saw a gigantic dead rattlesnake that he had killed in front of my doorway; it had bled out; that was what the blood was from. Then he informed me that this was the second rattlesnake that he had killed in front of my doorway that month. After that experience, I was told by a landscape friend that snakes never sleep and that they could be up and around at any time of the day or night. So my happiness and thankfulness for living in my condo in Bonsall started transitioning to fear, and I started searching for other places to live. The first place I looked at was in Carlsbad where my oldest daughter and her husband had lived for a while. It was beautiful. It was away from the sad memories, and it was still close and convenient enough for my family and friends. But from my research, I found that it was very expensive, and on my limited income, there was no way that I could afford rent of thousands per month. Even some of the areas away from the ocean or near the railroad tracks were not affordable. And I was still dealing with credit issues, which would make it hard for me to pass a credit check to secure a new apartment.

God had given me an opportunity to take a course called "It's Your Time" (IYT) offered by the Inland Empire Small Business Association. The course was women's entrepreneurial business training, and it came at the time right when I needed a very positive distraction from my sadness and misery after my separation. With my classes, I was frequently out late at night, so the thought of coming home, parking, and stepping on a snake was terrifying to me. I prayed about it, continued to be watchful and hopeful, but there was no real opportunity for me to move.

Then one day, I had another sequence of God events, which went something like this. I rarely went by our Fallbrook house because it was too sad and painful, and the house had a sense of emptiness or deadness to it. So, I tried to avoid it, but one day, the Lord directed me to go by the house at a time when I knew my husband was not there. Not only did I rarely go by the house, but I also rarely stopped at the mailbox to get the mail, but that day, I did. In the mail there was a statement from our investment company. We didn't have much. Mac had more in his IRA account than I had in mine—approximately five times as much. I had funded it during our marriage because he was older than me, and I assumed that he would need it before I did, but there was never enough extra money to fund both.

When we went through our divorce proceedings, the court forbade both of us from touching any of our assets until the Marital Settlement Agreement was completed. If I hadn't gone by the house that day and if I hadn't got the mail that day, I would never have known that my husband had disregarded the court order and removed $30,000 of our assets from our investment accounts. Around this same time, I received a phone call from a real estate agent in Idaho where we had a parcel of raw land that my husband had bought before we were married, which we finished paying off during our marriage. The real estate agent was asking me if he could list it. He mentioned that he thought he had a buyer and that there wasn't much real estate inventory at the time.

We listed the property, and it sold on the very first day. It was less than the amount of money that my husband had removed from our investments, but it was still a considerable chunk of money. With the statement, my attorney was able to go to the court and order that the monies from the sale of the Idaho property be frozen to equalize the money removed from our investment assets.

One day the paperwork had to be signed, notarized, and overnighted to Idaho for the sale to go through. The completed paperwork had to be there by closing on a Friday. I did not think that getting the forms notarized and overnighted to Idaho would be a problem. I went to the bank to get my papers notarized, and that triggered a feud between notaries in two states, and what I thought would take ten minutes, took hours. They argued over what kind of form to use, what was legal and what was not, what was acceptable and what was not. It was quite surprising. Finally, the paperwork was signed and notarized, and I walked from the bank across the parking lot to a mailing service center and told them I needed the paperwork overnighted to Idaho. The manager of the mailing service center said that the FedEx truck had already come and gone and that the earliest he could get the paperwork to Idaho would be Monday. That was not acceptable. It had to be there by Friday. I needed the sale to go through! He understood my situation and my distress, and he wrote an address on a sticky note. At 4:15 on Friday afternoon, he told me to go from Fallbrook to the UPS center in Oceanside before five o'clock.

I drove like a crazy person to get there before five o'clock when the UPS driver was scheduled to be at that center. But the address he gave me was incorrect, and Siri directed me to a beach house in Oceanside. So at seven minutes before five, I was not even in the right location. I plugged the FedEx office address into my maps and saw that it was seven minutes away. Once again, I drove like a crazy person to the FedEx center, ran into the store, butted in the line, and explained my situation to the girl at the counter. She threw me, the envelope that I needed frisbee-style, and told me that the driver was in his truck in the driveway. She told me to go flag him down. So I picked up the frisbeed envelope, ran outside, and stood in front of the FedEx truck, waving my arms in front of him. The driver got out of his truck. "What can I do for you, little lady?" he asked as he chomped on his gum. I explained to him that I had to get this paperwork overnight to Idaho. He said no problem. He took the paperwork and the envelope, compiled it, and said, "No problem; it is on its way." Whew!

After all that, I found myself in Oceanside exhausted from the events of the day. I had a counseling appointment to go to at seven that evening in Carlsbad. For the past year and a half, I had been having therapy sessions with a Christian counselor, who did not know my husband; he was helping me to heal and learn and grow. It seemed pointless for me to drive all the way back to Bonsall when I had to be in Carlsbad in two hours. So in my exhausted state, I drove to Carlsbad on the Pacific Coast Highway where there is a stretch of free parking along the coast just north of Tamarack. The most northern parking space was open, so I pulled in. I spent the next hour and a half to almost two hours just sitting on a concrete picnic bench meditating on the Lord and recovering from the day.

When it was time for me to go to my counseling appointment, I did an illegal U-turn right where I was parked. On Pacific Coast Highway, across the street from the Pacific Ocean, I saw a For Rent sign. I slowed down, snapped a picture of the sign on my phone, and went to my counseling appointment. The next day I called the number on the sign, and a woman answered the phone and informed me that she had many, many calls about the rental and for me not to even bother applying if I didn't have a perfect credit score. I told her that I had no idea what my credit score was, but it was unlikely that it was very good. She gave me a time to come back the next day to see the rental. She had two places for rent; I met her to look at the first unit, which was a larger guesthouse close to the ocean but not across the street. Afterward we went to the studio apartment that was above the carport; it had no view, but it was a place where I could hear and smell the ocean every minute of every day. The rent for this itty-bitty studio was the same amount I was paying for my condo; the studio was one room including a kitchen and a bathroom. The room felt like a hug.

Because the rent was the same as I was paying for my Bonsall condo, I knew I could swing it financially, and I told the landlady that I knew that I was supposed to be there. She tried to discourage me saying, "Oh, it's too small; it's so small." I just reiterated to her, "I am supposed to be here." She gave me an extensive application to fill out. To my recollection it was about four pages front and back. I took it with me and began to fill it out and realized that I did not have a lot of the information that the application required. I would have to go back home to get that information. She asked me when I was going to turn in the paperwork, and I told her that it would have to be the next day because I had to go home and get the rest of the information. She said, "Don't worry about filling the rest of it out. Just bring me what you have and a check for $25, so I can check your credit."

The next morning when I was back in my condo in Bonsall, I had another one of those very early morning awakenings and I decided that since I had a lot to do, I would not go back to sleep, I would get up and start my day. So I sat on the couch in the living room and tried to do my quiet time. But I had gotten up so early that I was having a hard time concentrating. I was having a hard time staying awake, so I leaned back on the couch and closed my eyes. I didn't really feel like I went back to sleep, but I had a dream. I dreamed that I woke up to the phone ringing and when I answered the phone, the woman on the other end said, "Your credit's crap." Then the next moment in real life, the phone rang, and I answered it.

It was the landlady. I was astounded that I had that preview of what was to come, and I didn't say a word.

I was very quiet, and her next words surprised me. She said, "I talked to the owner . . . ," and at the time I didn't know she was the owner. She continued, "I talked to the owner, and he said that if you pay a two-month security deposit, you can move into the studio apartment." So I told her that I would, and I did. I went from the terror of snakes in my condo in Bonsall to an upstairs studio apartment across the street from the Pacific Ocean. It was a very therapeutic location for me.

A few days after I moved in, I woke up and got out of bed only to collapse on the floor with pain in my right hip. I had no recollection of injuring it, so the pain was baffling. The hip was fussy after that day, and going up and down the stairs to my "hug" studio was sometimes difficult. About six months after I moved into my studio hug, I noticed that my neighbors in the ground floor unit were moving out. There were only two ground floor units of the six. All the other units were on the second story. AJ, the husband of the family with a young girl and a newborn baby told me, "You should move in here."

I decided to approach my landlords to inquire about the possibility. Prior to asking, I penciled out my budget to figure out what was the maximum rent that I could handle. If I remember correctly, the rent was around $2,400. My maximum ability to pay was $1,800. My landlady liked me and asked me how much I could afford. She lowered her price in increments until she landed on the $1,800 amount. I took that as an answer to my prayer and with the help of friends, I once again moved my belongings. On the first day that I lived downstairs, I opened the living room blinds and stared in utter amazement that I had an unobstructed view of the Pacific Ocean! I lived in that privileged place for six and a half years until an unfortunate raw sewage flood resulted in black mold and an unhealthy living environment.

SNAKES

When I think about the series of events that led to my living in that remarkable location, I see the snakes as God's impetus to relocate me. I could not have anticipated the gift that awaited me.

TRAIN ANGEL

When I converted our legal separation to a divorce, the court instructed us to sell our home in Fallbrook. When we separated, I chose to leave because my husband was partially running his mental health practice from our home office, and there would be no separation between us if he were coming every day to get patient charts and working with our part-time employees who did his insurance billing. We had purchased that house in 2002; it was a fixer-upper in an estate neighborhood and was listed significantly under market value when we purchased it.

We agreed that we would remodel it to bring it up to the neighborhood standards as an investment for our senior years. I had poured a lot of my time, energy, and creativity into remodeling that house. In addition, I had invested the inheritance that I received into the house and the remodel when my mother passed in 2005. So the court instructed us to sell the house. When it sold, I was to get my inheritance back, and we were to split whatever was over and above my inheritance. Agreeing on a real estate agent was combative, but I listened to a friend who counseled me to choose my battles, so I let my husband choose the listing agent.

The listing agent was a nice man whom we had known from our previous church; however, he did not live in the same town or community where our house was located. In fact, he lived almost an hour away. I had some very specific requests for any agent. For example, I requested signage at the entrance to our neighborhood and at our property location. I requested a presence in our local *Village News*, either in the paper or online, and I requested occasional open houses. I was assured that these requests would be complied with, but they never were.

One week I was even more physically and emotionally exhausted than usual. My middle son and his wife invited me to visit them at their home in Orange County and have dinner with them on a Friday evening. I was looking forward to spending time with them, and I took the train rather than drive because I was literally too exhausted to drive safely. So as I boarded the train from Oceanside on a Friday afternoon, I was very surprised that the train car was completely empty, but I didn't really think anything of it. I chose a seat at a table that had seating for four people. I chose that seat because it was on the west side of the train, and I would be able to relax and enjoy the beautiful view of the ocean for most of the hour-plus train ride.

Not long after the train started rolling Northbound, I started getting phone calls and texts from the real estate agent who was pressing me, after only ten days, to lower the price of the house by fifty thousand dollars. I had done a lot of research and spoken to a lot of other agents to find the right sale price for our property. I felt confident that the price that we were starting with was the right and fair price. So I was troubled when after a little over a week, he wanted to drastically reduce the price, and none of my requests had been implemented. There was no signage at the entrance, no sign at our property, no presence in the *Village News*, and no plans for an open house. He assured me that in today's world, the only way to sell a house is with online marketing. But to me a fifty-thousand-dollar price reduction was gigantic, and I didn't feel that any effort had been put forward to try to sell the house in those ten days. In addition to the texts and phone calls from the real estate agent, I started getting phone calls and texts from my husband; he was also pushing me to lower the price and berating me and calling me names when I resisted.

I was already exhausted, already emotionally thin, and this was a very difficult experience. So I lifted my eyes to the heavens and sent up a prayer, asking God what I should do, and I texted both the real estate agent and my husband in capital letters: "I – AM – NOT – READY – TO – LOWER – THE – PRICE." And I shut off my phone. Then, I folded my arms and laid my head and my arms on the table in front of me and said, "Oh, God, please help me not to be stupid." At the next stop an attractive young woman got on the train and sat across from me. At the next stop after that one, there were only two of us in the entire train car. A man wearing a business suit got on at the far end of the train car, and he proceeded to walk straight to where I was sitting at the table and asked if he could sit with me at the table. I remember thinking, "What the heck! First, there are many open seats. Why did he need to sit where I am sitting and then second, why didn't he sit with that cute girl across the aisle instead of at my table?" But no, he insisted on sitting at my table, and I didn't have the right to tell him that he could not sit there so I resignedly said yes.

Well, from the time he sat down, he immediately started talking nonstop, blah-blah, and I pointed at the quiet car sign that was hanging on the wall. He acknowledged the sign but instead of not talking, he just started talking in a whisper. Then I started getting very uncomfortable with the conversation as he was asking me a lot of personal questions. He asked me what I did for a living, where I lived, whether I frequently took this train route, whether I lived at the departing end or the arrival end, and on and on. So, I thought well, if I start asking him questions about himself, maybe he will stop asking personal questions.

I really didn't want to know about him, but I asked him where he lived and what he did for a living. And he told me that he lived in Escondido and that he was a real estate consultant . . . then suddenly, an invisible cloud enveloped me, and I was keenly aware that this was not a chance encounter! I looked at him and started laughing out loud, laughing so hard I had tears running down my face, and I looked at him and exclaimed, "Oh, I get it; you're not human; you're an angel!" He crossed his arms, smiled, and nodded his head in acknowledgement. So I started asking him questions. I asked, " So angel real estate consultant, can I ask you a question about my house?" And he again nodded in acknowledgement, and I began to describe my house and where it was located. He continually responded, "I am very aware of where your house is; I am very aware of your house, and I am very familiar with your neighborhood." So I said, "OK then, angel, the question is: 'Should I lower the price now?'" And he responded, "No, not for three months." This conversation was coming to an end because my stop for meeting with my children for dinner was coming up, so I asked, "Do you have a card?" He smiled at me and chuckled and he said, "I don't carry cards." As I stood up to get off the train at the stop, I said, "Well, goodbye, angel." And he said, "God bless you." I got off that train with a big smile on my face knowing full well that I had my first known encounter with a heavenly being.

I had grown up in the Roman Catholic church, and I never had any Bible training about angels. Of course, I had heard about them, particularly guardian angels. Once our pastor taught about angels not being cute little baby cherubs but fierce warriors who were terrifying. I knew from the Scriptures that we do encounter angels at times during our lives, and I knew for a fact that this was my encounter. When I have shared this God Story with my prayer partners, they typically ask, "Well, what happened? Did you sell the house?" I am sorry to report that we did not. Only months after we listed the house, my husband decided to stop making mortgage payments. That resulted in a short sale, and I lost my significant inheritance.

When I left my home, separated from Mac, and filed for divorce for the eventual end of my marriage, I had nothing. God has been faithful to provide for me as only He creatively can do over these past years. My faith has grown through all my trials, but I have genuinely rejoiced in meeting my train angel.

MAKEOVER

I believe this God Story will put a smile on your face. It reflects for me how much God cares about all the little details in our lives and knows all the hairs on our head. He is such a personal, loving God, and this is my story. In addition to being a mechanical engineer and a certified flight instructor and helicopter pilot, my oldest son is also an entrepreneur. He manufactures high-end coffee stations out of brushed metals and wood veneers and beautiful enamels; he sells them to organizations like Neiman-Marcus and Tesla. My son and his fiancé decided to throw a factory party for sales promotion and for family and friends to come and see and celebrate what they were doing. Well it had been a few years since I had purchased anything new, especially clothing. So, I was trying to figure out what on earth I would wear to this event. I was informed that my soon-to-be ex-husband was also going to be attending this event. I was nervous and uncomfortable; I was fearful of seeing him because I hadn't seen him for a very long time.

    If I was going to attend this event and I wanted to be there for my son, I wanted to go looking cute. So for the weeks prior to the factory party, I had planned to go shopping. However, because of one thing after another, I never made that happen. So there I was on the day of the factory event, which I remember was to start around six o'clock with a food truck followed by beverages and dancing. I had not been able to implement my good intentions, and I found myself trying to decide what to wear. I had decided that I was going to wear my best outfit—the one with that special top and the gold blazer. When I went to my closet, I couldn't believe that I had put the outfit in my closet with a big grease stain on the lapel. How did I miss that? Why would I put that outfit back in the closet without having it cleaned first? So, I had nothing that I felt comfortable wearing.

I left Carlsbad about ten o'clock on a Saturday morning, anticipating a six o'clock factory party. I threw a couple of things in my car that would do, and I was driving on the Interstate 5 Northbound. I had no plans or intentions of going shopping that day, but as I was driving Northbound, I saw signage for a shopping mall in the Mission Viejo area. I figured that I had a few hours to shop. I got off and followed the signs and arrows painted on the ground to a parking structure, winding around and around and up and up, until I finally parked at the entrance to a store without having any idea which store it was. I walked across a bridge several stories higher than the parking lot and into the department store only to realize that I had walked into Nordstroms.

Now, I only recall two occasions when I had shopped at Nordstrom's, and they were both times for Mother of the Bride or Mother of the Groom dresses for my adult children's weddings. I don't typically shop at Nordstrom's because they are very expensive, but where I walked into the store was the women's clothing department, and everywhere I looked were clearance racks, as far as the eye could see. I saw rack after rack with clearance signs, so I thought maybe I could afford something that was on clearance. So I started rifling through the racks, and I found a cute jacket in hunter green, and then I found that same jacket on another rack in beige, and then I found that same jacket on another rack in black. There

I stood holding these three fashionable jackets when a saleswoman approached me and asked if she could help by putting these jackets in the dressing room for me.

I said yes and handed her the jackets. When she returned, she asked if she could help me in any other way. Well, I am not a good shopper; I don't really like shopping, and I like shopping for myself even less; I had heard that Nordstrom's was known for having personal shoppers and helpful salespeople. So when she came back and asked me if she could help me one more time, I turned and looked at her and I stretched my arms out as if I were on the cross and I looked at her and I said, "Yes, dress me." I told her about the event that I was going to that night, and she kicked right into gear, knowing the level of stress that I was experiencing. She put me in a dressing room and proceeded to bring clothes to me. She never even asked me what my size was. She just brought in the clothes. The first thing that I put on was a pair of black almost bell-bottom pants that fit me like a glove. They were so comfortable and fit perfectly except that they were a little bit long.

Next, I tried on a beautiful fuchsia blouse that was made of crepe material. Those two garments alone made me feel cute, and when I put on the black jacket that I had found on the clearance rack, I knew that I had found the perfect outfit for the factory party. I asked the sales lady if there was any way that she could hem the pants immediately, and she said yes. She called for an alterations woman who was there within minutes; she measured my pant length and told me to come back in an hour, and she would have them hemmed for me. I asked the saleswoman if there was a place in the mall that did nails, and she assured me that there was. So while I waited for my pants to be altered, I went into the mall and hunted for a nail salon. They immediately waited on me, sat me at a manicure table, and gave me a perfect manicure in thirty minutes.

As I walked back to Nordstroms from the nail salon to retrieve my pants, I passed by a hair salon, and I thought, hmmm . . . could it be? So I went into the hair salon, asked if anyone was free; one of their most popular hair stylists, Taylor, happened to be available, and she went to work cutting, shaping, and styling my hair. While she was styling my hair, she asked about the event. She was very sympathetic about my concerns and asked me if I had an appointment anywhere to have my makeup done, and I kind of chuckled and said no. In fact, I was not used to wearing makeup because I usually have problems with eye styes whenever I wear eye makeup.

Well, she took it upon herself to call her girlfriend who worked in the cosmetic section at Nordstroms and asked if she was free to do my makeup for me, and she was. So I went from having my nails done to having my hair styled to meeting Taylor's friend who did my makeup—for free! While her friend was doing my makeup and making me cute, she asked me what shoes I was going to be wearing with my new outfit and I pointed to the shoes I was wearing, which looked like black flat ballerina slippers. She just shook her head and said, "No, no. You can't wear those." And so when she finished with my makeup, she walked me to the shoe department at Nordstroms and basically like Vanna White spread her arm around and asked, "Do you see anything that you like?"

I pointed to a pair of ankle-high, pointed-toe boots. I always liked boots on other women, but I had not owned a pair of boots since my honeymoon because they never really fit comfortably with my thick ankles. So she sat me down and had one of the shoe salespeople bring me boots and put them on my feet, and they fit like bedroom slippers. They fit so perfectly that the anatomy of my ankles was not an issue. So now I had my nails done, my hair styled, makeup, and new boots in hand when I went back upstairs to retrieve my altered pants.

I got to the factory party all dolled up. I got out of my car a little bit late, but I arrived in time to see my middle son and his wife in the parking lot. When I walked up to them, they didn't even seem to recognize me. Then, I spoke, and my son's fiancé said, "Oh, I didn't recognize you." I said, "Well, I really wanted to come looking cute!" And she said to me, "Well, mission accomplished!"

I was bathed in prayer through the whole factory party, and I had peace and calm and joy that only comes from the enduring power of the Holy Spirit. When I look back on that day, I kind of shake my head and smile. Anytime we women try to coordinate something like that makeover, it is usually complicated and disappointing. This was a God makeover. It wasn't anything I had planned or scheduled. To coordinate all those people, all those services, the way that it came together was a hug from God for me, telling me, "I am here; I love you; I care about all the little details of your life." Years later, I still wear those pants, that fuchsia blouse, and those boots. I still feel cute and still remember that He truly cares for me even in the details of my life.

NOT ALONE

Since 1971, when I was nineteen years of age, I have had two dads. I met my adopted dad, Ike, when I was thirteen years of age. He was married to Maurine, my second cousin once removed. Maurine's mother was my grandfather's sister. I was thirteen years old when my mother drove us to Glendora to meet her relatives. I still remember what I was wearing that day, a yellow tent dress with white polka dots and white lipstick, which was the fashion at the time. I remember pulling up to their house and seeing acres of citrus orchards across from their home.

It was love at first meeting on both sides. I immediately felt a bond with Maurine and Ike, and they felt a bond with me. When I started dental hygiene school in Pasadena later that year, our relationship grew deeply. I believe God provided them in my life for support when my own parents chose not to be involved with me. My parents divorced when I was twelve; it was a very difficult divorce. My mother never fully recovered from that divorce, becoming what I would later understand to be a man-hater. In addition, she was full of bitterness about having been taken away from her home in New Braunfels, Texas, when she was a child.

My biological father could most accurately be described with the term *gigolo*. He was a man of passion and addiction. He was addicted to prescription drugs, alcohol, and sex. I never had a very good relationship with my dad mostly because he was not an honorable man, and I did not respect him. Ike was a retired US Marine Corps colonel, and he became the functioning father in my life; he became my protector; Ike and Maurine exemplified unconditional love for me.

My mother passed away from lymphoma in 2005. Maurine passed away in January 2012. Ike passed away in January 2016, and my biological father passed away in April 2017. These people and these dates are integral to a complicated interwoven God Story.

For eighteen years prior to my mother's death, we did not talk to each other. That was her choice, not mine. When she was diagnosed with lymphoma, my brother contacted us sisters to inform us that she was ill even though she had instructed him not to tell any of us. She didn't want any of us to know until she was "dead and gone." When my brother informed me of her condition, I disregarded her wishes and showed up, along with my sister, Rose, while my mother was having chemotherapy. She lived approximately three hours from where we lived.

For the last five months of her life, my family and I cared for her until she passed into eternity. In December that year, God orchestrated an unprecedented time of forgiveness and reconciliation, and I was there with her when she died. During those five months of being with her, she asked me several questions—mostly questions about what was going to happen to her after she died. I knew from experience with her that I shouldn't answer those questions in my own strength or my own opinion, so I sought wise counsel, did some biblical research, and collected answers to her questions, but she was not strong enough to have that conversation until the week prior to her death while she was on hospice.

I had previously committed to throwing a birthday party for Ike. My mother had stopped eating the Tuesday before the weekend. The birthday party was scheduled for Sunday. We had spent a lot of time together over the previous weeks and months, and I felt that we had made our peace; we had asked each other for forgiveness. If I could be there when she passed, so be it; if I could not be there, so be it. On Sunday morning, the day of Ike's scheduled birthday party, in the wee hours of the morning, one of my five children came down with the stomach flu. One after another came down with the stomach flu. By morning we had to cancel the birthday party because most, if not all, the kids were sick. Since the birthday party got canceled, I decided to drive to the San Fernando Valley where my mother was on hospice care to see her for what I thought might be the very last time. I remember driving northbound in traffic so thick that I could have walked there faster. I called and asked my husband and children to pray for the parting of the Red Sea, the traffic sea of cars, and almost immediately the traffic dramatically dissipated, and I was able to drive to the San Fernando Valley quickly.

My sister Rose from San Francisco was there and so was my brother from the San Fernando Valley; our sister Annette was not. When I walked in, Rose said, "She is still alive, but she has been waiting for something or someone." My brother Andrew was sitting in a chair in the corner of her room when I came in. I walked over to my mom's bedside, and I told her that I was there and that I was there to answer all the questions that she had asked me over the past five months. So, I started reading from the Scriptures; I would quote her question and then read God's answer to her question from the Scriptures. On the very last question—on the very last verse—she took her very last breath. We felt her spirit leave her; her empty, tortured shell of a body was all that was left. My brother, who I do not think was a believer at the time, stood up and exclaimed, "Oh my gosh, Mom waited for you to get here. She waited for you to answer her questions!"

Now fast-forward seven years. For several years prior to 2012, my dear Maurine suffered from senior dementia or Alzheimer's. Maurine and I were kindred spirits. Her mother and my mother were clones of each other even though they were a generation apart.

When I lived with Ike and Maurine in Glendora for two years, we would sit for hours, night after night comparing our experiences and our childhoods, which were almost identical even though we were from different generations. We genuinely loved one another and enjoyed each other's company. I was already struggling with biological depression, which was a side effect of the catheter ablation procedure used to treat my cardiac arrythmias in December 2011. So, when Maurine got pneumonia on a Friday and died the following Monday, I had a really difficult time losing her. She was a very special person in my life, and losing her only exacerbated my depression. Over the next two years, Ike truly was the father I never had. We talked for hours while he was at his board and care; I was experiencing my painful separation, which would ultimately become my catastrophic divorce.

Ike and Maurine were the grandparents that my children never had from their biological grandparents. My precious Ike passed away in January 2016 leaving a huge irreparable hole in my heart.

For eleven years I had Durable Power of Attorney for Healthcare for my biological father. Despite the lack of relationship between us and his not being an honorable man, I took my responsibilities as his health-care advocate very seriously. At some point during those eleven years, my oldest daughter asked me why I was caring for him when he had not been a very good father or very moral person, and I responded, "It's my duty; it is because I am a Christian."

I sat with my biological father for hours before he passed away in April 2017. It was a sad time for me because I realized that, with his death, he would never be the father that I wanted, needed, and hoped he would be. My entire life from childhood until then had been punctuated with profound seasons of aloneness, and losing these four people just exacerbated those feelings.

As a sidenote, for most of my adult life, my sisters, Rose and Annette, chose to reject me as their sister and did not want to be in a relationship. Envy, jealousy, and pride can cause people to make ugly choices. I still remember the time that Rose told me to my face that she hated me, first because I had all those children and she had none, and second, because I was a Christian and had raised her nieces and nephews as Christians. To this day, Rose pursues relationships with my children, intentionally circumventing any relationship with me. It hurts my heart to this day, but, if being in relationship with my children, who love God, will influence her for His kingdom, then I suffer with purpose. It has taken me decades to learn that I cannot influence anyone to love me or care for me. Relationships are complicated. We can't force people to respond in a certain way. There are times when we just don't understand, and there are no answers. But God calls us to trust Him, be joyful and full of gratitude despite our circumstances. I do not like it, but I am learning to accept it.

Incidents following our dad's death made this even more evident. It was my legal responsibility to inform all three of my siblings when our father died. They all knew that his death was looming on the horizon, but when I called to tell them that he was gone, they refused to answer their phones or talk to me.

I always wondered how I would feel when my dad was gone, wondered if I would even shed a tear. So, I was surprised and caught off guard when, on the drive home after he passed, I lost it. I was crying so hard I couldn't see how to drive. It was dark, nighttime, dinnertime, and I decided that it wasn't safe for me to drive in that condition. So I pulled off the road through the rain of my tears, and I saw a familiar restaurant through the darkness, a Cheesecake Factory, which was located at the same mall where I had shopped for the factory party. I went inside and ordered dinner and a martini. I assumed I would just wait until I was in better condition to drive when I could drive safely. I was in no hurry, and I was very emotional; the waitress was very concerned for me. She kept coming by and asking me if there was anything she could do, asking me what was wrong. I finally felt strong enough to share with her that my father had just passed away about an hour earlier.

My personal, compassionate, and comforting God sent me to that restaurant at that time for Colleen to be my waitress. She later told me that she had stepped aside and prayed for me while I was there in my tearful distress, and she had gone around to the other servers and collected money from them to pay for my dinner. So there I was in the Cheesecake Factory crying, waiting to be safe enough to drive, when God sent me Colleen to comfort me and to provide for me. That was completely unexpected, but it was God's way of putting His arms around me and letting me know that I was not alone.

The next day I decided to eat lunch close by where I was living; that was only the second time I had ever been to this restaurant called The Islands. I was by myself, sitting in a booth, and a peppy little waitress took my order and then she came back and unexpectedly sat in the booth across from me asking me how she could comfort me. Her name was Marissa, and she explained that she used to be a student at Biola University at the same time some of my sons were students there. I marveled that within forty-eight hours, God sent me Colleen and Marissa; then that afternoon He also sent me Erin.

In my emotional pain, I was somewhat robotic, just functioning, and I needed to run an errand at the local Costco, which was very close to The Islands restaurant. I ran my errand and was walking toward my car in the Costco parking lot when a Costco employee whose name badge read "Erin" approached me. Out of the blue, Erin came up to me and said, "You need a hug," and he put his arms around me and gave me a random hug in the parking lot of Costco!

You might remember that I mentioned earlier that God sometimes communicates to me in *threes*. This was a very important and dramatic illustration of His love and compassion and involvement in my life. Perhaps if those three people had been familiar to me, it wouldn't have been as evident to me that it was from God. He ministered to me at a very difficult and painful time—first through Colleen, then through Marissa, and finally through Erin's hug.

I am very much aware that God has no time constraints. To my knowledge only we humans, on planet Earth, have time limitations. So even though I have memories of my parents and of Maurine and Ike, years have gone by since they have been gone. The memories all blur together to remind me that God is truly God and that He is truly personal, relational, and detailed in His ministry to us, to me. So, even though this journey of relationships has sometimes been difficult, I am thankful that He is personal in my life and that I am *never* alone.

Finally, I recognize and acknowledge my paternal and maternal legacy for "grudge holding," hatred, intolerance, and unforgiveness. I observed these traits throughout my childhood and into adulthood with certain family members. They exercised much judgment and extended very little grace to one another or even to other people. One of the hugest God transformations in my life has been a willingness to forgive and extend grace. It is also one of the most difficult lessons that I have ever had to tackle.

THE TICKET

Maurine and Ike have two sons, Thom and Rik. Thom is married to Jennifer. When Ike died, Thom, as the older son, was the designated trustee of his estate. With that huge responsibility, he asked his brother Rik and me, the unofficially adopted daughter, to plan Ike's memorial service. Even though Ike passed away in January, his service was not scheduled until April. Because he was a retired US Marine Corps colonel, he was entitled to military honors at his service, and it took until April to schedule a time for military honors to be presented.

Ike and Maurine had lived at an incremental care facility in Riverside. I lived in Carlsbad, and Rik lived in San Francisco. My youngest son was going to graduate school in Berkeley. So, to meet with my cousin Rik who lived in San Francisco and plan Ike's memorial service, I decided to pack my car with Ike's memorabilia and drive to San Francisco. I would also have the bonus of visiting with my youngest son.

The planning session with my cousin and the visit with my son went very well, but the timing of it could not have been worse. As we planned Ike's memorial service, I was getting telephone calls regarding my biological dad who needed to go on hospice. The calls were from the board and care where he resided in Sherman Oaks and also from his Medicare and Medicare supplement insurance companies. After planning Ike's service, I had to drive from the Bay area to the San Fernando Valley to sign paperwork for my dad to go on hospice. It was a very busy, difficult, and emotional time. I decided to drive back to Southern California via the California coastline because I love seeing God's majestic creation. As I was driving south from the Bay area, I received a barrage of phone calls about my dad and his needed care.

It was hard to pay attention to the driving because I was so distracted with the conversations. I realized that I most likely had missed the turn for the California coastline as I was driving through the farmland and agricultural fields south of Gilroy. I was feeling lost, trying to get my bearings, while at the same time getting a phone call from my dad's medical insurance. The woman from the insurance company was not very nice. She was very aggressive and very assertive and demanded that I make certain immediate arrangements. In hindsight, I should have pulled over and stopped instead of trying to manage all this while driving. But I had time pressures as I was trying to get to the San Fernando Valley quickly, so I unwisely chose to keep driving instead of stopping.

I was having a heated conversation with the woman from Blue Cross when I saw in my rearview mirror the flashing lights of a police car behind me. As I pulled over on the shoulder and rolled down my passenger window I continued speaking on the hands-free Bluetooth in the car. The woman from Blue Cross was still talking. I reached into my purse, retrieved my driver's license out of my wallet, reached into my glove box, and pulled out my registration and insurance papers—all the while the woman was still talking. I was pantomiming to the police officer while telling this woman that I needed to hang up and that I would call her back later.

But she did not relent. It was evident to the police officer that the situation was not normal. She finally hung up, and the police officer said, "It is my duty as a police officer to ask you what is going

THE TICKET

on in your life that caused you to drive ninety miles an hour?" Well, I was shocked that I was driving ninety miles an hour. I had no idea. I didn't even know that my four-cylinder Honda CRV could go that fast. But apparently in my heated discussion, I drove faster and faster. I explained to him that I was just leaving the Bay area after planning my adopted dad's memorial service and that I was driving south to sign papers to put my biological father on hospice. When I said those words, I started crying.

He told me that frequently when he stops people to give them tickets, they start crying but that this time, he didn't think that it was a ploy; he believed me. I begged him not to give me a ticket. I told him that I had gotten a speeding ticket less than a year ago in Washington state, and I was told that if I did not get a ticket in any state for one year, that ticket would be erased. I was only weeks away from having that ticket removed from my record.

I begged him, but he said the best he could do would be to reduce my speed from ninety miles an hour to only five miles an hour over the speed limit and at least that would reduce the cost of my ticket. Again I pleaded with him telling him that it wouldn't help me because if he gave me a ticket, I would get the Washington State ticket too. He apologized. He was very compassionate, but he said that there was nothing he could do and that I should expect to get my traffic ticket in the mail in thirty days.

I waited thirty days and never received the ticket. Another thirty days went by. No ticket. Those thirty days became months. And the months became years. My all-powerful, Creator God erased both tickets.

Now in comparison to the other God storys, this one is tiny. But it's the tiny ones that make me feel the most loved. It's the tiny ones that help me to know God knows me personally and that He really cares about me and all the little details of my life. I don't understand what happened or how He did it, but I know in my heart that God obliterated that ticket just for me.

NOY

The Thai Kitchen (TK) was a legit Thai restaurant in Temecula about twenty minutes north of Fallbrook. It's owner, Noy, is from Thailand. TK has the best Thai food of any Thai restaurant ever. Our family has eaten there for probably two decades. I don't remember when I first met Noy or when we first started eating at her restaurant, but in time Noy and I became friends. Noy had a sad story. She was married to an American, and she was very much in love with him. They ran the restaurant together. One day, they had driven to work in separate cars, and he left to go home first and then she followed later. When she got home, he wasn't home, which was baffling because he had left first.

According to her story, she retraced the route he would take from the restaurant to home, and she discovered that he had driven off the road and was dead. Noy was always reserved but friendly and always classy and beautiful every time we ate at her restaurant. We became friends, and I invited her to visit me at my home in Fallbrook. I remember the one time she came. She brought food from the restaurant, and we feasted on yellow curry. In hindsight, I probably moved too quickly to share about my relationship with God with her. Instead of our friendship deepening after that luncheon, there seemed to be some distance between us.

Fast-forward to the weekend in April of Ike's memorial service. I had been in Riverside, setting up for the service, which was to be held that coming Sunday. I was exhausted—physically and emotionally. This was a big undertaking, and many people would attend Ike's service the next day. All I wanted to do was to go home and go to bed. I wasn't hungry. I didn't have an appetite. I really didn't feel like doing anything except going home. As I was driving southbound from Riverside back to Bonsall, it was almost as if my car had a mind of its own. Instead of driving home, I felt compelled to go to the Thai restaurant, and my car practically drove itself there. Now I wasn't hungry, I didn't have an appetite, I didn't want to eat, but I sat in a booth and ordered my favorite dish.

What happened next was unusual. Noy came to my table. In the past, she would stop at my table and visit in passing, but this time she sat in the booth with me—across from me. I could tell that she was troubled. She shared with me that this was the last weekend that her restaurant would be open; she would be closing the restaurant on Monday. I was so surprised and disappointed. This was my favorite Thai restaurant ever. I asked her why, and she shared that she had gotten in trouble with the IRS. Because she was Thai and didn't speak good English, she had not responded correctly to the IRS, and they had taken all her money out of her bank account. And she would not be able to pay her rent on Monday morning. The shopping center showed no mercy, no grace. The rent had to be paid on Monday, or the restaurant would be shut down. I asked her how much she needed to pay the rent, and she said she needed $5,000.

Now in January that year, I had my taxes done. I always have them done in January because for years I had college students who needed FAFSA forms filled out early in the year, so I always had my taxes done early. That year, my CPA told me that I was going to get an unexpected tax refund of approximately $1,000. Of course I was looking forward to getting that refund, but when it came, for some reason I was too busy to open the envelope right away. Days or even weeks went by before I opened the envelope, assuming that I was getting a refund from the IRS. Well, to my shock and awe, when I finally opened that envelope the refund check was not for $1,000. It was $6,600, and I was stunned. I was shocked. I called the CPA and asked him if there was a mistake, and he assured me there was no mistake. He had not figured the return precisely when I was in the office, but this refund was truly mine.

Well, after I paid his fees and tithed, I had in my hand $5,000, which I kept in cash just in case of an emergency. Now sitting in Thai Kitchen across from Noy, I had one of those invisible clouds from the Holy Spirit descend on me, and I immediately knew *why* I had been given that tax refund. It was for such a time as this. But I felt very possessive of that money. I did not have any discretionary income, and I felt like I needed that $5,000 to help pay my living expenses. So, I was very resistant when God called me to help Noy. I was sure I was misinterpreting what I was hearing. Certainly, God was not instructing me to give Noy, whom I didn't really know very well, that kind of money. So, I left the restaurant without saying anything and without offering any help.

But on the way home and later that night I felt the prick of conviction. I knew that God was pressing me to help Noy. But since I was resisting His directive, I decided to put out a fleece, or my version of the ancient Urim and Thummim, for God to prove to me that this was real, that this was what He wanted me to do. I was so resistant. My fleece was this, "God, tomorrow on my way from Bonsall to Riverside to Ike's memorial service, I will stop by the Thai restaurant with the $5,000. If Noy is there, I will know that you want me to give the money to her. Now Noy had told me the night before that she was not planning to be at the restaurant that day, so I felt pretty safe with this fleece.

I called the restaurant, and she wasn't there. I went into the restaurant, and she wasn't there, and the staff told me she was not coming in that day. So as I was leaving the restaurant and getting ready to go to Riverside to Ike's memorial service, my hand was on the handle of the restaurant door to pull the door open to leave, and Noy's hand was on the other side of the door pulling on the handle to open the door. I exclaimed, "Oh, I thought you weren't supposed to be here!" She said, "I wasn't. I just stopped by to pick something up that I forgot." At that moment I *knew* that God wanted me to give Noy the $5,000.

I asked Noy to come into my office, which was my car; I sat in the driver's seat, and she sat in the passenger seat, and I pulled out the envelope of cash and handed it to her. I told her, "God wants you to have this." She opened the envelope and saw the cash and burst into tears. She said that she had been praying for help and that she knew that this was God's answer to her prayer.

I told her that we were not going to draw up any kind of paperwork or a loan document, but that if it was possible in the future, I would appreciate her paying me back. There was no official paperwork, no interest, just giving her the money at that time.

Noy paid me back every penny of the money over time, and she and I have become good friends—the kind of friends that are like sisters. She and I really enjoy spending time together and the relationship that we have built has given me an open door, an opportunity, to share my life and my relationship with God with her openly. She loves me like a sister. She has offered for me to live with her in my senior years since I have no financial nest egg because of my divorce. She has a house in Thailand complete with servants, and she has offered for me to go to Thailand either to visit or to live with her.

I did not expect that tax refund, and I felt very possessive of it when it came. Letting go of that $5,000 out of my tight fists was hard. But the gift and trust of Noy was worth every penny of that sacrifice and that test. This was one of the boldest times that God communicated what he desired from me. And even though I flunked in my initial response, I am glad that I ultimately relented in obedience, for I would not have experienced all of God's faithfulness and the sweet, sweet friendship that I now enjoy with Noy.

CHRISTINE

I had no idea when I met Christine that she would be an integral part of my grieving the loss of my Ike. I met Christine while taking a course at the University of California San Diego (UCSD). It was her first time attending and was my second. I had been asked to help with students who were taking a course in orofacial myofunctional therapy, and Christine was a dentist from Juneau, Alaska. She sat in the first row on the left-hand side all by herself. After a day, it didn't seem like she was interacting with the students very much. I knew the Lord was prompting me to be intentional about initiating a conversation with her.

When I found out that she did not have a car and was staying in the dorms, for the last two days of the course, I invited her to join me for dinner in the surrounding area of La Jolla. I mentioned that I was from the San Diego area and that I knew my way around. I told her that she was welcome to join me if she would like to eat somewhere other than the school cafeteria; and she did.

The first time we went out to dinner, we were joined by another student. At the restaurant, Christine shared that she had recently lost one of her two daughters; her daughter had been studying in New York to be a chef. She had a rare medical condition and because of her medication, she was not supposed to drink alcohol. However, her daughter was at a social event with friends, and she was encouraged to have just one small drink . . . and her daughter never woke up that night from her sleep.

It was this first encounter with Christine that was a traumatic bonding experience for us. After those dinners and after the course ended, Christine and I frequently talked and became good long-distance friends. We had a lot in common in dentistry even though she was a dentist, and I was a dental hygienist and myofunctional therapist. She knew that I had never been to Alaska. She also knew I was going through a very difficult time in my marriage, which ended in a separation and divorce. She knew that I really enjoyed experiencing the beauty and wonder of God's creation. So over the next several months, she suggested that I come visit her in Alaska, and she offered to pay for my trip.

She suggested that we schedule the trip sometime after the winter ended as it would be easier and more enjoyable to get around without snow. To my recollection, in December 2015, she called one Sunday afternoon, told me to get my calendar out, and we planned for me to visit her in Juneau, Alaska, in April 2016. She made arrangements for my flight. You might remember that Ike passed away in January 2016. His memorial service was scheduled for April 2016. Before Ike passed away, Christine had already planned, paid, and scheduled for me to visit her in Juneau, Alaska, only two days after Ike's memorial service. So forty-eight hours after Ike's memorial service, I found myself on an airplane heading to Juneau, Alaska.

Christine had me stay with her and her husband at their home, which overlooked the most photographed glacier in North America. Her house was set up high, and every day, the eagles flew by her windows. She was a hospitable hostess, and twenty minutes after my arrival, she offered me a job in her office as a dental hygienist. Now I did not have license to practice in Alaska, so that was not feasible. But it was a privilege and an extreme compliment to be asked. As I recall, I was there for about five days, staying with her in her home the whole time, and every day she had something different for me to do.

The first day, we went on a beautiful hike in pouring rain. Halfway into the hike, she yelped and exclaimed, "Oh, my gosh, I forgot the bear spray!" And I was somewhat taken aback thinking, "Do we need bear spray?" And so she began to tell me what to do in case we encountered a bear. Two days after Ike's service, she flew me to Alaska, housed me, fed me, entertained me, and showed me sweet, sweet friendship. Two days before the end of my visit, she handed me the keys to her truck. She said she had to go to work that day in the office, and I could have her truck and go exploring in Juneau while she was at work; and so I did. That exploration, as much as I enjoyed it and appreciated it, only cemented my knowing that I did not want to live in Alaska. It was too wild for me. As a senior single female, I did not feel that Alaska was the place for me. I didn't feel comfortable not being able to go up the driveway to get the mail out of the mailbox for fear of being attacked by a bear. I wasn't comfortable seeing her small dogs outside for fear of that one would be kidnapped by an eagle. It was too wild for me.

Midway through my visit, she scheduled and paid for me to go at five in the morning on a ferry that went by water to the cities of Haines and Skagway and one or two other places. That day on the ferry was the most emotional and meaningful day for me since Ike's memorial service. The water was smooth. It was a beautiful day, and the surrounding scenery was jaw-dropping, gaspingly beautiful. Everywhere I looked was evidence of God's majesty. It was a unique and special alone time with God. It was a healing time for my heart. Christine couldn't have known when she scheduled it months earlier what an important, healing day that would be for me.

I took photos of a mother and baby moose in Haines and saw totem poles in Skagway. I was in awe, loving my time with the Lord, relishing the staggering majestic beauty. The ferry was not going to return to Juneau for another day. So, Christine arranged for a private pontoon pilot to pick me up in Skagway and fly me back to

Juneau in time for dinner. On that day I was able to see the beauty at ground level from the water and beauty from the air as we flew from Skagway back to Juneau.

When I had the truck and was exploring Juneau on my own, it was a rainy day. I didn't have the proper outerwear, so Christine lent me one of her husband's waterproof parkas to wear while I was exploring.

I wanted to go to a place that was somewhat of a nursery and had places to walk around and look at beautiful plants. I didn't want my cloth purse to get wet in the rain, so I took my driver's license and debit card out of my wallet, and I put them in the pocket of Steve's jacket. That night we had our final dinner together, and I packed and prepared for the flight home the next day. When I got to the airport, I was completely confused as to where my driver's license and credit card were.

I had no recollection of where I had put my driver's license and debit card. At the airport I was searching for them in my purse and in my wallet. Fortunately, I had my passport with me, so I was allowed to board the plane. But I opened my suitcase and searched through my suitcase looking for my driver's license and my debit card. By then, I was very hungry, and I was looking forward to purchasing some food either at the airport or on the airplane. It wasn't until I was boarding the plane that I remembered that my driver's license and debit card were still in Steve's jacket back at Christine's house. So I was boarding a plane with no driver's license, and I couldn't buy any food. I had a boarding pass with a seat assignment that was confusing me.

I showed the boarding pass to the attendant and asked her, "Where is this seat? I am not familiar with this numbering." And she said, "Your right here . . . in first class." Christine had surprised me with the generous gift of flying me home first class. Now, do you know how much the food costs in first class? Well, if you don't, let me tell you, it is free; so, although I did not have my debit card, I was able to eat on the flight home.

In first class there are only two seats side-by-side, and a woman sat next to me—to the left of me. I was working on my laptop, and she looked over and saw photos of mouths on my laptop. She leaned over and asked me if I was an orthodontist. I told her I was not, and she told me that she used to be a dental assistant for an orthodontist. We struck up a conversation. I asked her where she was going, and she said San Diego. She was from Anchorage, Alaska. Her husband had grown up in San Diego. His family of doctors still lived in San Diego, and she and her husband had lived in Alaska for over forty years but had always planned to move back to San Diego to live closer to his family when they retired. So she was flying from Anchorage to San Diego for the sole purpose of buying a house that next day. Now my house had just recently been put on the market, and the house that she was planning to purchase sounded like the description of my house. I asked her where the house that she was planning to buy was located, and she said it was in Fallbrook. Well, I could hardly believe what I was hearing.

I described my house to her and told her the street that I lived on, and she said, "Oh, I know exactly where your house is. I looked at a house on that street. But it was earlier in the block, not at the end of the street." And she told me, "I had no idea that your house was for sale on that street." So with all the challenges I had with my real estate agent not having the listing well-advertised or the signage well positioned, it frustrated me to know that she was looking for a house just like the one that I was selling, and had been on my street and never knew that my house was for sale. I happened to have a flyer from my house sale with me that I took to show Christine and her husband, so I gave the flyer to this woman.

No, she did not buy my house. She never even went to look at my house. We never spoke again, but I was in awe that only days after

Ike's service, Christine had already arranged for me to fly to Juneau, Alaska. She housed me in her home, showed me hospitality, fed me, entertained me, put me on a ferry to look at God's majesty, sent me home on a plane so I could see God's majesty from the air, and then gifted me by sending me home first-class. I am convinced that only God can orchestrate these types of events in life. And there I was sitting next to a woman from Anchorage who was on her way to San Diego to buy a house in Fallbrook. I don't believe in coincidences, only God-instances. And this was a huge one for me.

GABRIELLE

Over fifty years ago, I was working as a dental hygienist in a dental office in Glendora. I was cleaning a beautiful young woman's teeth when she started to cry. I was concerned that I might be hurting her, so I stopped and asked, "Did I hurt you? Are you okay?" And she said, "No. It's not you. It's just that right before I left to come here, my husband informed me that he was divorcing me and marrying my best girlfriend." Well, of course, she was devastated.

From that moment on, we became friends. I took her to church with me, and we have been friends and stayed in touch ever since. She remarried and moved to Oregon, but we have remained in touch all these many years. When I was going through my separation and divorce, I didn't exactly want to write a Christmas letter to everyone updating them on what was going on. My not-so-subtle way to communicate the situation was to send a Christmas photo of me with my kids without my husband in the picture.

Several people figured it out; Gabrielle was one of them. I received a phone call from Gabrielle because she was concerned. She loved me and invited me to come visit her in Oregon. She said she would take care of me. She was now widowed. I did not have the money to go to Oregon, but once again God creatively provided that for me. A few weeks after her invitation, I was visiting Dawn in Colorado and attending a conference in Denver. Everything I did was on a very tight budget.

I was leaving the conference in Denver, but my flight was not going out until the next day. However, the airport shuttle from Denver to the airport was very expensive. I had an opportunity to join a group of conference attendees in an airport shuttle that would reduce my cost of the shuttle greatly. So I decided to go and stay at a hotel near the airport rather than staying at the hotel where the conference was located. So, I found myself in the backseat of a suburban, which was the airport transport, squished between three other women. I knew none of the women in the shuttle, but they were all leaving from the conference. The woman to my right asked me where I lived and what I did. I told her I lived in San Diego and that I was a dental hygienist and a myofunctional therapist. She was ecstatic about meeting me. She told me that she was a speech and language pathologist in Medford, Oregon, and that she had a speech and language pathology practice with employees who worked with her.

She asked me if I would consider going to Medford to teach her staff an overview of myofunctional therapy. I told her that I would be willing to do that; I had done presentations and teaching in the past, and she offered to pay for my airline ticket to Medford.

That was God's way of creatively providing for me to go visit Gabrielle who lived thirty minutes from Medford. After I taught in Medford, I visited Gabrielle for approximately five days during which Gabrielle talked a lot about her memories of fleeing communist Hungary when she was twenty years old. I had a delightful, restful visit with Gabrielle, but at the end of the five days, I said, "Gabrielle, if you miss Hungary so much, you should go back for a visit. You're not dead yet."

That was in December 2016. I did not know how old Gabrielle was; she was one of those beautiful ageless Zsa-Zsa Gabor type of Hungarians. She was very spunky and active with a very sharp mind.

She told me she would be turning eighty on her next birthday. Every month she would call me and ask me if I thought she could really do it—if she could really go back to Hungary for a visit. Every month I told her, "Yes, if you really want to go, you should go." This was a recurring conversation every month until June. In June, she called me and said that she had decided to go if I agreed to go with her. She wanted to go for an entire month and had already thought through and planned all the different places she wanted to go in Hungary, all the different foods she wanted to eat, and all the people she wanted to visit. She asked if I would go with her and said she would be willing to purchase my airline ticket. I thought to myself, "Hungary, where is Hungary? Do I want to go to Hungary? Is Hungary beautiful?" I told Gabrielle I would pray about it, think about it, and get back to her. When I prayed about it, God impressed upon me to say yes; He gave me the green light. So Gabrielle started planning, and I was simply to be her traveling companion.

A few weeks before we left in September 2017, three things happened. I was working as a temp dental hygienist in a dental office in Fallbrook. I had been working in that office for nine years temping for the four hygienists when they needed a substitute. The income was inconsistent but helpful. I was a little concerned about going out of the country without a credit card. I had debit cards, but I had no credit card, and after the divorce, my credit was such that I could not get one. I applied to different online banking institutions and was rejected by all of them. The first of the *three* events involved a dental hygiene patient named Nadia. Nadia was a person of authority with Point Loma Credit Union. We struck up a conversation while I was cleaning her teeth, and when I casually explained my dilemma, she offered to help me get a secured credit card for the trip.

Either that same day or within a short period of time, another dental patient named Tom mentioned, as I was cleaning his teeth, that he used to live in Slovenia. Now to my knowledge, I had never had a patient from Slovenia or at least not one that mentioned it during their appointment. In his friendliness, he offered to give me his cell phone number, so that I could call or text with any travel questions about the area since Slovenia was a neighboring country to Hungary.

The third of God's *three* events was a telephone call from a man named Roger. Roger was a well-respected health professional and colleague living on the East Coast; he was a specialist in breathing. I had spoken with Roger on multiple occasions at different conferences when we attended the same courses. The phone call from Roger went something like this, "I'm trying to email you something, and it keeps bouncing back. Do you have a valid email address?"

So of course I gave him my email address. I asked him at the time what he was sending me. He mentioned that he was sending me a course opportunity, and I asked him when the course would be held, and he said it would be in September. So, I said, "Well then, never mind because I won't be here. I'll be out of the country." He asked me, "Where are you going? I told him I was going to Budapest, Hungary. He exclaimed, "Oh, if you're going to Budapest, then you need to look up Dr. Gabor. He's an orthodontist in Budapest who knows what we know and does what we do." I told him, "No, no, no, I'm going as a traveling companion. I'm not going for work, but thank you very much. And Roger proceeded to email me Dr. Gabor's contact information despite my disinterested response.

On the first or second day of September 2017, Gabrielle flew from Medford, Oregon, to Toronto, Canada. I flew from LAX to Toronto, Canada, and we met at the boarding gate in Toronto. Gabrielle and I had to go through a customs gate to board. We had forms to fill out and potential possessions to declare. I remember that we were really pressed for time, and it was a very chaotic and confusing interaction. The terminal was very far away from where the plane would depart, and we were tight on time.

GABRIELLE

I carried a backpack and a briefcase. I was trying to help Gabrielle fill out her forms in addition to doing my own, but Gabrielle was confused and got argumentative with the customs officer. He became angry and threatened her. With our tight timeframe, we did not need any time delays. We finally got the customs issue resolved, but we literally had to do the *running through the airport to get to the gate* routine that you see oftentimes in the movies. An airport shuttle passed us by, and we flagged it down; the shuttle had room for Gabrielle, so she went on the shuttle ahead of me to the gate.

As I started jogging to the gate as best I could, I panicked when I realized that I had left my rolling suitcase at the customs gate and no longer had it with me. I was halfway to the terminal, and I didn't have time to go back and get it. So instead of running back, I just started walking back because I knew that there was no way I was going to retrieve my suitcase and get to the gate on time. I was resigned to missing the flight. I turned around and started walking back to retrieve my suitcase and within seconds, a male voice said to me, "Are you Victorya?" I was so shocked. I looked up and saw an airport assistant who had my suitcase. After I left customs, he had followed me with my suitcase after realizing that I had left it behind. But my question has always been, how did he know I was Victorya? There were many female travelers. I retrieved my suitcase and continued running to the gate; Gabrielle and I were the last two passengers to board. They had held the plane for us, and we then began our flight to Budapest, Hungary.

Gabrielle had everything planned and reserved for our trip to Budapest. We had a reservation for three nights at the Hotel Gellert, which was a famous spa hotel. Gabrielle claimed that she was familiar with Budapest public transportation; however, it had been several years since she had been there. For two or three days, we only left the hotel to walk down the street to get dinner. I realized that some sort of emotional paralysis had set in for Gabrielle, and she seemed incapable of making decisions about where to go and what to do.

On day three, I recalled that Roger had emailed me contact information for the orthodontist, and I was ready to get out of the hotel and do something different. So, I asked Gabrielle if she would mind if I taxied to meet with Dr. Gabor. She was amenable to that, so I emailed Dr. Gabor mentioning our mutual colleague, Roger, and asked him if I could come to his office in Budapest to meet him and see his office. He immediately replied via email that he was not in Budapest; he and his daughter were traveling in San Diego, California. In fact, they were staying with a mutual friend and colleague in Fallbrook, California. What were the chances of that? They were in my own backyard while I was in Hungary! But he invited me to go to his office and meet his myofunctional therapist, Geri. I went by taxi to Dr. Gabor's office and met Geri.

Geri was a speech and language pathologist trained in myofunctional therapy, and she was very gracious in showing me around the office and explaining what she does with her patients. I was only with Geri about thirty minutes when I realized that she knew something that I didn't know, something that myofunctional therapists don't do in the United States. Her way of doing therapy is much more multisensory including much more proprioception. I asked Geri how I could learn what she did, and she told me that she would be teaching her first course in English from September 29 to October 6. I told her that Gabrielle and I were planning to return to the United States on September 28, one day before her course would begin. But I felt that what she knew was very important to my being a better therapist.

As I taxied back to meet Gabrielle, I thought about it and decided that it didn't make sense to go back to Hungary at another time to take the course. I was already there. So, when I got back to the hotel, I told Gabrielle about Geri and the course, and she and I agreed that since we were both flying home to different destinations anyway (her to Oregon and me to California), she was fine with me changing my reservation and flying home after the course.

Since Gabrielle seemed to be experiencing some paralysis with moving forward in her visit to Hungary, I suggested that we purchase one of those red double-decker step-on-step-off bus tours of Budapest, so that we could get the lay of the land and see what was where and figure out what she wanted to do. At first she was resistant, assuring me that she had it all under control, but she relented, and we bought a two-day pass for $13 each. The pass included a two-hour tour step-on-step-off of Budapest along with a Danube River cruise. That night we talked about our plans for the following day, and we agreed that we were going to get on the bus and go from the beginning all the way to the end without getting off just to get the lay of the land. Then, we would take the Danube River cruise and have dinner on the Danube River.

The next morning, after having a wonderful breakfast at the hotel, we crossed the street and boarded the double-decker bus. However, instead of taking the bus all the way to the end as we planned, somewhere around the third stop, Gabrielle stood up on the bus and got off at the Castle District waving her cane at me to get off with her. So, there was a spontaneous change of plans without any communication. I suggested that we take the shuttle to the top of the Castle District, which was several stories. I don't know how tall it was, but it was very high. For all I knew, it could have been thirty stories high, and it was layer upon layer of medieval stone and uneven steps, and it was quite steep to walk up.

I was concerned for Gabrielle with her pain issues. As we went to board the shuttle, we were waved off by a man who said it would cost us seven euros to ride to the top. Gabrielle wasn't willing to spend the euros and decided that she wanted us to walk, and so we did. She made comments along the way about how she had played on those steps as a child. So, I was glad that we could be in a location that was familiar to her and where she was happy to be back. I could tell from Gabrielle's face that she was very tired and that she was in pain when we arrived at the top. We arrived at one end and then had to walk all the way to the other end before making our way down and back to the bus. The top of the Castle District is like a little community or city of its own, complete with restaurants and stores and shops. So, we walked in and saw some of the sites before we headed back to the bus stop.

I suggested we take a taxi or a bus down, knowing how tired Gabrielle was, but she refused. She assured me that she knew how to get down. It was a maze of stone streets and steps. I would ask taxi drivers and bus drivers for directions just to keep us on course. But as we got to the bottom, closer to the bus stop to get back to continue our tour, she instructed me to go stand and wait for the bus, and she sat on a bench to rest and wait. So, I did. As I was standing at the bus stop looking to my left for the red double-decker bus, only seconds later, I heard the roar of a screaming crowd. I turned my head to look and saw a group of people around someone, and I realized that it was Gabrielle. She had fallen down a flight of stairs and hit her head on the railing, and the crowd had screamed and was trying to help pick her up. When I got to her side, she was very disoriented. She did not know who I was, nor did she know who she was.

The crowd was mostly made up of tourists. Budapest locals were not very friendly to tourists. One young girl, Agnes, who was a tour guide came to our rescue. She was Hungarian, but she spoke exceptionally good English. It took four phone calls and a two-hour wait before an ambulance arrived to transport Gabrielle to a local hospital. We were taken to *San Janos*, which is Saint John's Hospital. It was a nightmare! Before we left on our trip, I insisted that we both purchase travel insurance and that I be given the contact information for Gabrielle's two adult children. I immediately contacted the insurance company and Gabrielle's adult children. In broken English, the emergency room doctor informed me that Gabrielle had to have emergency hip surgery and that time was of the essence. When I asked him what he was planning to do, he erupted in anger yelling at me saying, "I am the doctor! I am the doctor!" He wasn't used to having anyone ask him any questions; he expected everyone to confer all authority to him. They would not let me stay with Gabrielle, and they wheeled her off on a gurney to be prepared for surgery.

I made my way back via Budapest public transportation to the Hotel Gellert where Gabrielle and I had been staying. I had done no research about Hungary or Budapest because I was going to be a traveling companion to Gabrielle. Finding my way around in a non-English speaking country was very challenging.

Gabrielle had her hip surgery while I was back at the Hotel Gellert. I returned to the hospital around nine in the evening with some of Gabrielle's things. The hospital was more of a compound than a single building; there were many buildings on site. I had no idea where to look for her; there was no staff. No one spoke English. No one knew where she was. I called the Hotel Gellert and asked them to send an English-speaking taxi driver to meet me at the hospital compound. The taxi driver was very helpful as we went from building to building to look for her. The hospital building was old; there was evidence of a previous war and potholes in the hallways, and some of the ceilings were crumbling. Finally, we found Gabrielle on an upper floor in a ward with eight other women; she was lying in the bed asleep and naked. She had no sheets, no blankets, no hospital gown. I did not know that the hospital did not provide those basic needs. I did not know to pay or bribe the staff. Early the next day I took public transportation to a local mall to buy her a robe and a blanket. Gabrielle remained in the hospital recovering for about ten days. The food they served her was disgusting; the soup looked like dishpan water, so I brought her food from outside.

The Hotel Gellert was some distance from the hospital, and it was expensive, so I relocated to a pension within walking distance of the hospital. I was unsure and insecure about the safety of the area as there was painted graffiti along my walking pathway going and coming. One night I had dinner at a Hungarian restaurant that was on the way to the hospital from my pension. During my meal, I became very emotional and started to cry. The owner sat with me and comforted me and had me leave with a small red ceramic covered pot that I treasure today.

When Gabrielle was able, our travel insurance sent a courier from the United States to bring her back to the US, and I found myself alone in Budapest, Hungary, a place that I knew almost nothing about. I texted my friends and prayer partners and asked for help. I received a response from Licia, one of my myofunctional therapy instructors. We had become colleagues and friends. She was born and raised in Italy and enjoyed dual citizenship. She was at her home in Italy and suggested that I rent a car, drive over the Alps, and stay with her until my course began in Budapest. I rented a tiny, stick shift car and drove in the pouring rain, between semitrucks to her home north of Venice. We enjoyed our visit until day two when we were having dinner, and her sister burst through the front door screaming in Italian! Their brother, who lived next door, had a heart attack and died. It was a horrible, traumatic occurrence for everyone. I felt I was an intruder during a very personal family time and wanted to give them their privacy. Late that night, Licia brought a map to my room, telling me I would need to leave because family would be arriving for the funeral. She circled places on the map that she thought I would like to see in Italy, Croatia, and Slovenia. I found myself following her recommendations on the map. I traveled her dot-to-dot route mostly in the pouring down rain.

The first stop in Italy was a beautiful castle hanging over the sea. When I came around the corner in the parking lot, the rain stopped, the sun came out, and I gasped out loud at the magnificent sight! I toured the castle and stayed in an Airbnb that night. The people were friendlier than in Budapest. The countryside and towns were colorful, beautiful with many new sights, smells, and foods.

For the first three days, I felt a little fearful and anxious, thinking that if anything happened to me, no one, including my children, would know where I was. On day three, as I was driving in the rain to Croatia, I was aware of the presence of the Lord. A peace came over me, and I knew that the entire experience was no coincidence. All the happenings were His divine orchestration for *"such a time as this"* (Esther 4:14). I no longer had any fear; instead I relished the God journey, at times talking out loud to Him, my constant travel companion. It became a treasured me and God trip!

However, crossing the border into Croatia was terrifying. I was the only car. There was no signage, so I did not know that I was at a border. After examining my passport, the stern guard told me that I needed to pay an exorbitant amount of money to pass. I lifted my eyes to the heavens, asking God, "What do I do?" God prompted me to tell the guard that I was unable to pay. I was concerned, especially since I was alone, but the guard looked at me, annoyed, then raised the arm, and let me pass. Once again, I was aware of God's presence and grateful for His deliverance.

Croatia was jaw-dropping majestic in its beauty. Again, I stayed at an Airbnb and ate dinner at a sidewalk restaurant on the water where the waiter said the fish had just been caught. As I was eating, I remembered my dental patient from Slovenia, who had given me his telephone number. Since I had an international phone plan, I messaged him and he responded with recommendations for me to go to Postonja, Slovenia. Postonja is known for having the largest castle in a rock in Europe and also for having impressive underground caves. I drove to Postonja and again stayed in an Airbnb located in the countryside.

The young man who was managing the room gave me a recommendation for where to eat; the restaurant was a fifteen to twenty minute drive. When I arrived, the large, multiroomed restaurant was empty except for a hostess who seated me. I ordered a pizza and waited, alone in the room, for it to be served. Just as the pizza arrived, I heard voices of additional guests arriving, including a couple who spoke English! Even though we were on opposite sides of the room, I could hear their conversation. They were hungry and ready to eat, and I was very excited to meet some English-speaking people, so I picked up my pizza, walked over to them, and offered to share it. They were welcoming and invited me to join them, and we shared my pizza and ordered wine. We talked for a very long time about a variety of topics. Gideon was an anthropology professor at the University in Jerusalem, and both he and Neta were second or third generation Holocaust survivors. We talked about our travels, our families, and about God. They were on holiday, traveling north to south; I was traveling south to north. They made some wonderful travel recommendations, sharing their telephone number for me to call if I had any questions.

The pension they recommended was wonderful. The basement was a bakery where the traditional Slovenian gingerbread heart-shaped, mirrored, cookies were made. The young woman who kept the tradition had a fiancé who played the accordion, and they sang for me.

I made my way back to Budapest, returned my rental car, and stayed in an Airbnb near public transportation to and from the myofunctional therapy course. Originally, the course had five people registered, but by day one, people dropped out until I was the only attendee. The speech and language pathologist instructor and I became fast friends, with me helping her with her English and her sharing about her taste for the delicacy of cooked "brains"! We called ourselves "brain buddies." The course was pivotal to my knowledge and practice of myofunctional therapy. In addition to learning from Geri, I had the privilege of learning from Alexander who came from London to teach about "Voice Gym." They implement "myo" differently in Europe than in the United States, incorporating a more sensory integrative approach to therapy.

This God Story was my biggest most life-affecting story to date. I remain friends and colleagues with Geri and Alexander, and Gabrielle and I remain friends. She later needed to have her hip surgery redone, but she has recovered well.

Spoiler Alert: Later, I realized that this trip was a prequel to my Israel trip.

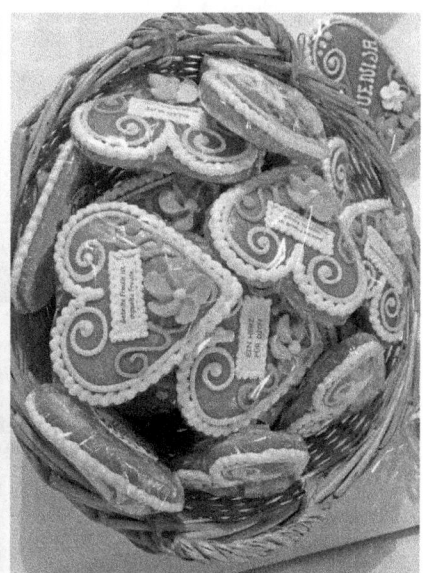

ISRAEL

After I moved to Carlsbad, one of the elders from the church I attended in Escondido (a different church from the one my husband and I had attended) gave me a list of churches to visit, but I had not gotten around to doing that. Over the years, I have attended a variety of churches, usually with my children or friends. In July 2013, I was asleep and awakened by a God Tap. I knew He was directing me to go to church that day. Even though I had the list of churches that I was intending to visit, He directed me to attend a different church that day, Carlsbad Community Church on Harding Street. I remember thinking that church was not on my list, but without a shadow of a doubt, I knew that was where He was directing me to attend.

As far as I was aware, I did not know anyone who attended there. When I arrived, I sat in the middle section up close to the front, so I wouldn't be distracted during worship. That service was a very emotional time for me; the songs, hymns, and the sermon ministered to my soul, and I found myself weeping through most of the service. I sat in the middle of the row, and there were two senior couples one on each end. During the meet and greet time, I stood up and introduced myself to the couple on my right and then I stood up to greet the man on my left whose wife had gotten up to greet other people. When I walked up, I read his name tag, and I was surprised to recognize an old homeschool family friend named Bill. I was surprised to see him sitting in the same row that I was sitting in, and then his wife Mary appeared, and she said, "What are you doing here?" That first visit turned out to be a kind of reunion. I knew that was where God wanted me to attend as my church home.

I attended infrequently for about six months mostly because I was out of town or out of the country for a considerable amount of time. Two things happened within days or weeks of the time I returned from Hungary in early October. While I was in Hungary, the dentist where I had worked as a dental hygiene temp for the past nine years sold the practice to a young dentist who was just out of dental school. I knew Jordan, but he asked to talk with me when I got back. In the meeting he informed me that I would no longer be temping in that office as my passion for airway dentistry did not match his paradigm or goals for his new dental practice. He was very complimentary about my work and wrote me a very good letter of recommendation; however, I found myself concerned about my financial situation.

Then weeks later when I was attending a church service at Carlsbad Community Church, I wasn't particularly paying attention to the announcements because I wasn't a regular attender nor was I plugged into any of the ministries at that point. So, when the pastor announced to the congregation that they had opened four new spots for people to join them for a ten-day trip to Israel, I was surprised when the Lord directed me that I was to go on that trip. I immediately argued with God in my head. I had just returned from Hungary, and I was hoping not to go anywhere for a long time especially somewhere they did not speak English. I could not afford to go; I didn't have the money, and I had just lost my temp position. I only had a few thousand dollars in savings, and that would be needed to supplement my living expenses. But God was pressing me to go; not only was I to go, but I sensed there was some connection between the Hungary trip and the Israel trip, which made absolutely no sense to me at all. I thought that maybe this was a part of God's helping me have closure from my divorce because my husband and I had gone to Greece, Egypt, Turkey, and Israel on our honeymoon, and I had noticed that I had experienced several instances over the past year that I considered times of closure. God once again ministered to me in *threes*. First, family friends, Gordon and Gail, felt led to send me a check for $750. Second, the travel insurance paid me for all the expenses incurred with Gabrielle's accident. Last, I was rifling through a box of paperwork, and in between the pages, I found two one-hundred-dollar bills.

I knew that God was directing me to go on this trip, but I didn't understand why, and with trepidation I handed over the money to go on this new God-venture. If I remember correctly, about twenty-six of us from the church signed up for the ten-day Israel trip. I knew no one. I wanted to get to know some of the people before spending ten days with them, so with my God-given administrative skills and gift of hospitality, I hosted two luncheons for the people on our trip—one at the church and one at a local Dennys restaurant.

This was another faith-deepening God-venture for me as there definitely were times of closure. I remember standing near the aqueduct in Caesarea, Israel, surprised that even after thirty-four years, I remembered being there on my honeymoon. I had no roommate, but for every meal I sat with a different couple or family from our church on the trip.

There were three unmarried women and three unmarried men on the trip. The three men were all widowers. One of the three women was a widow, one had never been married, and I was the third unmarried woman—divorced. We were a busload of brothers and sisters in the Lord; it was a wonderful time of

Christian fellowship together. I was full of joy and happiness, and people would comment about my smile; I felt like the weight of the world had lifted off my shoulders, and I was so very happy to be there. The first night in Israel, they switched the destination of our original planned trip, and we spent the first night at the Dead Sea. I remember waking up early because it is a different time zone from the US. It was early morning hours, and I felt led to go out to the Dead Sea from our hotel. It was remarkable that no one was there.

It was just God and me looking at sunrise over the Dead Sea. It was a beautiful time of intimate prayer and worship, and then toward the end of the trip, we completed our tour in Jerusalem. I took one day away from the tour group and taxied to Tel Aviv to spend the day with Dr. Ayal who was a colleague and dentist. We spent the day together working on pediatric patients and examining oral ties in patients. Toward the last night in Jerusalem, God pricked my memory, and I remembered that the couple I had met over truffle pizza in Slovenia lived in Jerusalem and, in checking my phone, I did in fact have a telephone number for one of them. I texted them and within seconds of my text, I got a response wanting to connect with me, inviting me to their home, and offering to share a meal with me. The weather was pouring rain, and I suggested that they come to the hotel where I was staying and be my guest for dinner. I anticipated another delightful time of friendly conversation over our dinner meal, but what ensued genuinely surprised me. I had asked my new friends to pray for me while I met with my guests for dinner; several of them met Neta and Gideon when they arrived at the hotel. So, Neta, Gideon, and I went into the dining room, and I was not able to take a bite of food for three and a half hours. Both Gideon and Neta peppered me with questions about Christianity, about the person of Jesus Christ, about the end times. I wasn't sure that I had my own understanding and firm theological convictions of how to answer some of the questions they asked me. But God did a supernatural job of answering their questions. Right before they left, Gideon asked me a most amazing question, "Can a man have a relationship with God like you do, or is it only for females?" To this day, I marvel at such profound questions. I said goodbye to them at the hotel. As they were going to their car in the pouring rain, I was exhilarated but exhausted from the three-and-a-half-hour conversation and decided to go up to my hotel room even though I hadn't eaten dinner. As my finger was reaching to press the elevator button, the Holy Spirit came upon me and impressed upon me that this was why He sent me to Israel . . . for such a time as this. At that moment I clearly understood the connection between the Hungary trip and the Israel trip. I clearly understood that God had sent me according to His will and His sovereign purpose to have that three-and-a-half-hour conversation with Neta and Gideon. I have not continued to communicate with them since that night, but I continue to diligently pray to the Lord on their behalf. So much of the time when God directs me, I am resistant. Sometimes, it is only after the event that I see His sovereign purpose.

Forgive me, Lord, for being resistant; please help me to obey without resistance. In the last communication that I had with Gideon, he encouraged me to write out my God Storys. This book is also a response to Gideon's encouragement.

JACK

All twenty-six of us who were on that ten-day Israel trip have become bosom buddies. When we were on the trip, I used to refer to us as "bus buddies." Even though we did not have assigned seating, just like at church, people usually sit in the same seats or the same pews all the time. We sat in the same place on the bus for those ten days. Behind me sat Nick; in front of me sat Lila, and to my right across the aisle sat Jack. Behind Jack sat Colleen, and on and on. When we returned home from Israel and arrived at LAX, we once again took our positions on the bus bringing us from LA back to Carlsbad, and we sat in the same places as we did on the bus in Israel.

While he was in Jerusalem, Jack had his cell phone pickpocketed and in order for him to continue communicating with his daughter, he had me text his daughter Polly whenever he wanted her to know what he was doing or that he was safe. While we were on the bus returning to Carlsbad, Polly texted me to inform Jack that while he was gone, one of his closest friends had passed away. Jack was very emotional, and I felt sorry for him, so I patted the seat next to me on my bus bench, so he didn't have to sit alone since he was so emotional and upset. After sitting next to me for a while and composing himself, at some point on the way home, he turned to me and in a loud voice, that everyone on the bus could hear, asked, "If I asked you out, would you go out with me?" Well, I was completely caught off guard; I did not see that coming. And at that time in my life, I wasn't considering dating or looking for a new relationship. I was still recovering, healing, and growing from my trauma with my divorce, but I knew everyone on the bus was listening to hear my answer, and so I scurried to think of an acceptable answer and quickly came up with, "Well, if it is for friendship . . ." So, we got back to Carlsbad and unloaded our suitcases, and everyone transitioned from being out of the country for ten days in a different time zone.

Within the next couple of weeks, I started thinking about Jack's invitation, and I started to panic. I wasn't interested in dating; I wasn't interested in another relationship; I took it to the Lord and prayed about it, and I felt the Lord directing me to write a letter to Jack, basically telling him about my past and sort of a *you don't want me*, kind of a message, which we later called the Go Away Jack letter. The letter was long and comprehensive, and it revealed my past marriages and traumas and childhood experiences. Before I gave it to Jack, I shared it with my Christian counselor in Carlsbad, and he applauded me for writing it. He felt that I had done an excellent job relaying information and that it was a good, healing exercise for me to do.

Then I delivered it to Jack but knew that he would have some comments or questions. It was not the kind of letter that you could have a five-minute conversation about. So, I suggested to him that we spend several hours together where we could have an opportunity to talk. I suggested that we have what I call a "P and P day." He agreed and asked me, "What is a P and P day?" And I informed him that I had made it up and that it basically means, "I plan. You pay." He laughed, thought that was funny and agreed to meet, so we scheduled a time on the calendar. I intentionally scheduled a P and P day as a small test. If I was going to consider dating him or anyone else, I wanted to know about his attitude toward money, and I wanted to know if he could physically keep up with me given our age difference of eleven years. Without explanation, I gave him an address, and he met me at a donut shop in Carlsbad.

From the donut shop we walked to the train station, and I gently instructed him to purchase two one-way train tickets to the San Diego Santa Fe station. While were taking the train south to San Diego, Jack surprised me. After reading my letter and praying over it multiple times, he had clearly and concisely dissected it into three portions. He cut off the top half, he cut off the bottom half, and just like a surgeon he reattached them so there was no way of knowing that they had originally been separate documents. He taped the middle section, which was my past, and he stapled it shut on all four sides. On the train traveling south, he handed the letter back to me and said, "I don't care." This was a shock to me. I was sure the information in that letter would be a Go Away Jack message. It surprised me that my past was not an issue to him. We spent the day together—a lot of walking, a lot of talking; we had lunch on the water at my favorite restaurant, The Fish Market. We walked to Seaport Village and to the Ferry Landing where we bought two one-way ferry tickets to Coronado, and we walked and talked on Coronado. Then we had dinner on Coronado while watching the sunset. From there we walked to downtown Coronado, where we watched a live performance opening night at the Lambs Players. At the end of that performance, we hailed an Uber and we Ubered home.

It was a long but fun day getting to know each other, but I was still only interested in friendship.

If I recall about two months later, I was visiting Jon and Kathy, friends in Hollywood whom I had known for over forty years. They are both dear friends, and I have a key to their house and a room of my own. I was sleeping there one morning when I got a God Tap. God woke me up, and I knew he was directing me to write out something. I got out a legal pad of paper and a pencil and just started writing as He was filling my mind with questions. I wrote like water pouring out of a pitcher . . . question after question after question. When He was done, there was a total of thirty questions. I knew I was supposed to give those questions to Jack. All the questions reflected God's standard for a Christian relationship or Christian marriage. These were questions about headship, salvation, and spiritual leadership. So, I obediently emailed the questions to Jack, feeling like, well if that first letter didn't have him go away, then these thirty questions certainly will! But they didn't.

I kept pushing Jack away, telling him that I needed space, I needed time, I was healing. It was a constant conversation of Go Away Jack.

Then, in May 2018, my youngest daughter graduated from college. The whole family came together for her graduation, and my youngest son came to visit me at my Carlsbad home for three days after graduation. During that three-day visit, my son, who was soon to graduate with his PsyD degree, specializing in child psychology from a school in Berkeley, informed me what he had been learning as a psychology student. He had been thinking about me and concerned about me. He told me that over the years, he had seen patients who had a fraction of the trauma that I had experienced who couldn't get out of bed in the morning. He was concerned that my chronic pain and health conditions were somehow related to my unresolved personal traumas.

Initially, I dismissed the conversation. It was sweet for the first thirty minutes, and then after a while it got really irritating, as my son was psychoanalyzing me, his mother.

What ensued after this was the most dramatic of God's directing me in *threes*. Following my son's concern for my past traumas and health, I had two additional events occur. I was doing intensive coursework with a health-care professional in Phoenix, Arizona, and she informed me during the functional neurological intensive that my past was adversely affecting my present. My birth history was such that I had been born dead. I was informed that this birth trauma had affected me my entire life, so much so that my autonomic nervous system, my sympathetic, and my parasympathetic, had never integrated.

So, without considering all the other life traumas that I had experienced, this birth trauma seemed to be a big deal affecting my health. A lack of neurological integration affects emotions, causing them to be either flat or hyper emotional. The third of the three God events was a new functional gastroenterologist whom I was consulting in Hillcrest. I had only two visits with her, the first visit of which was almost four hours long. In that time, she developed a treatment plan that required extensive bloodwork, which she scheduled so I would have the results at the next appointment soon after I returned from that intensive in Arizona. So, I showed up for my gastroenterologist appointment, affectionately calling her my "gut doctor," expecting typical or traditional lab results, but she specializes in a technique called Endobiogeny. With this specialty she plugged the results of the bloodwork into an algorithm on her computer and then proceeded to present an integrative whole-body condition report.

I was completely surprised when, as she was reading the results of my lab work, she said almost verbatim what the functional neurologist said in Phoenix. She said that I did not have an integrated autonomic nervous system and that my sympathetic and parasympathetic systems were working independently of each other and that the problems with my gut and chronic pain were a result of unresolved past traumas in my life. I was shocked. That was not anything I was aware of nor was it anything that I would have even considered in the past. But the way God got my attention once again with his *threes* made me start to pay attention. My son got involved in helping me. He did research to find therapists in my area who understood this lack of integration and who specialize in therapy techniques, one of which was called somatic experience.

I went to the pastor of my church, relayed all this information to him asking him his opinion of all this, and he surprised me by saying, "If you had come to me and told me you had cancer, then I would expect you to go to an oncologist. If you have this condition because of past trauma, then you should go to the specialist who can help you resolve it. And if you can't afford to pay for proper treatment because insurance doesn't cover it, we will help you." I was stunned with this knowledge and their willingness to help me. I knew in my heart that this was the direction God was leading me.

My son found a therapist in Oceanside. I went to him for three sessions. At the first session, when I walked in and met him, I knew immediately that this was not where I was supposed to be. Toward the end of that first session, he shared his anger at God for allowing his wife to get cancer, and I knew I was there as a messenger, not as a patient. In my third and final visit with this therapist, he asked me to relay how it went when I visited my close friend in Oregon who was battling cancer and when I visited my oldest daughter and her family. I relayed the information he requested, but I realized looking at my watch that I still had a good amount of time left in the session and I didn't really have anything else to talk about. So, I did a quick inventory in my mind and realized that I wanted to update him about Jack.

I started to tell him all the reasons why I should not be dating anyone: How I was in the process of healing. How I was resolving past traumas. How I wasn't interested in a new relationship. As I started ticking off all these things, he sat across from me in his overstuffed chair with his arms and legs crossed and a big smile on his face, nodding his head. And then, as I was talking, as I was ticking off all these reasons, the Holy Spirit, that invisible cloud, came upon me, and I sensed Him impress upon me, "Get to know the person you are saying no to. Maybe you are supposed to go through all these things with someone by your side."

I remember the therapist smiling and nodding, but I was not looking at the therapist; I had my head crooked looking up and over my right shoulder having an inaudible conversation with God. "Really, God? Jack?" By the time I left counseling that day, I knew God was directing me to date Jack and to get to know him, so I called Jack on my way home and asked him if we could talk. He met me across the street from my home and we sat on a concrete bench overlooking the Pacific Ocean and talked. When I told him about these events and that God had instructed me to date him, he cried and told me that he didn't think he would ever hear me say that . . . and that he was really happy. The date was July 10th.

The functional neurologist in Arizona had cautioned me not to make any changes or any big decisions for three months while I was undergoing therapy. So, I asked Jack to move slowly.

It surprised me how compatible we were. We laughed and laughed and laughed. We enjoyed each other's company, we finished each other's sentences, said the same words at the same time, liked the same foods—unusual things that most people don't like at all, like chicken livers. I could feel Jack's love for me. He did not have to say anything, and I found myself falling in love with him at sixty-six years of age when he was seventy-seven. He would say to me, "I feel like a teenager again." And I would agree. Jack and I met in January 2018 on the Israel trip, and for six months, I basically told him, "Go away, Jack." Over the next six months, Jack proposed marriage and then rescinded his proposal three or four times.

The first time he rescinded his proposal and broke up with me was because I thought too deeply. The next time was because he was concerned that he would not be able to be the spiritual leader that I hoped for. The final time was because his daughters and sons-in-law gave him an ultimatum saying that if he remarried, he would no longer be welcome in their homes and he would no longer be considered part of their family. Jack had been married to his daughters' mother for over fifty years; they could not fathom seeing him with someone else. They had not adequately grieved her passing. Jack broke up with me out of fear, telling me that his family came first.

I felt betrayed. I felt abandoned. I was devastated, but Jack was a gift from God. He came into my life when I was insecure—at a time when I felt that I was not valuable and that I didn't have anything to contribute to a relationship. Jack showed me that I could be loved and that I could love again.

Jack and I had met Bob and Ruthie and their son Joel on the Israel trip, and we had all become friends. I enjoyed watching Joel on occasion while Bob and Ruthie would go out on a date. Among a few other things, Jack had gifted me with tickets to the symphony. However, he had not given me the tickets at the time but told me they were coming. After we broke up, I asked him if I would still receive the tickets, and he said, "Yes, I will get them to you." So, I arranged to go to the symphony with Ruthie on a Saturday night. Ruthie volunteered to drive us to the San Diego Symphony, and I offered to cook us a nice dinner, so neither of us would have to incur the expense of going out to a fancy restaurant. We got all dressed up cute and fancy, and then Ruthie came over to my home for dinner before we left.

As the two of us were eating, having a glass of wine, and enjoying each other's company, I blurted out, "Oh!"

Ruthie looked at me inquisitively, "What was that? What is going on?"

And I said to her, "Oh no!"

And she asked, "What?"

And I said, "God is directing me to write a letter to Jack's daughters. Oh no. I don't want to do that. Why would I want to do that?"

And Ruthie sat across the table from me, clapping her hands together kind of moving up and down in her seat going, "Goody, goody, goody. I get to watch a God story in process."

I tried to ignore the directive, but as I was riding with Ruthie to the symphony, God was writing a letter in my mind. I could almost see typewriter keys tapping out words on paper in my mind. Then as we got to the symphony, still more words were being written on a page in my mind's eye. Driving home from the symphony . . . still more typewriter keys tapping. We arrived home late, and Ruthie suggested that instead of going home right away, we sit and listen to the ocean waves and have a last glass of wine before she went home. We sat and talked until 1:30 a.m. I am too old for that, and I was exhausted; I had a delightful time, but I was ready to go to bed. At 1:30 a.m. as I crawled into my bed, I got the God Tap. The impression was . . . "Excuse me? Excuse me? Did you forget to write My letter?" I knew it was pointless to argue with God, so I got up, gave Him my fingers, and His words poured out onto the paper. I never changed a word. Everything was written perfectly.

I printed three copies: one for Jack, one for his daughter Polly, and one for his daughter Hannah. At church the next morning, I saw Jack. We were not supposed to sit together; I was planning to sit with other friends from the Israel trip who happened to be in the choir. While I was waiting for them, Jack relocated his belongings and came and sat next to me. I remember the inquisitive look on Sharon's face when she came to sit with me, and I just shrugged my shoulders. After church, Jack said that he had planned to talk to me but that he did not really have anything new to say. I told him that I did have something to tell him, and I asked when and where he would like to talk.

He said he could talk then and offered to go to my home to talk. I said that was fine. When he arrived, I told him how God had instructed me to write the letter to his daughters the night before. I gave him a copy of the letter and told him that while he read it, I would go into the kitchen and empty the dishwasher. Halfway through the letter, I could hear him crying. When he came into the kitchen, he told me the letter was perfect. It was exactly what he needed. He had been praying and asking for God's intervention and that letter was it. I asked him what he planned to do with the letter. Was he going to snail mail it, email it, or hand carry it? He said he was going to see Polly that afternoon and he was going to hand carry it to her, and that he would hand carry a copy of it to Hannah on his way to Polly's. However, Jack had one request. I asked him what his request was. He asked me to go with him to deliver the letters, and I said no. I did not want to do that. He insisted, saying that this letter was from both of us and that we should both deliver it. After listening to his perspective, I agreed to go, but I told him that I was not going to do the talking.

We arrived at Hannah's house first. Jack had recently moved in to live with Hannah, so with his key he let himself in, and I walked in behind him. Hannah stood in the doorway of the kitchen and told us that she did not appreciate being surprised. Her husband Stan who was sitting in the living room next to the door grumbled when I walked in. Jack offered the letter and asked them to read it. Stan said, "That's not going to happen," and walked out of the room. Hannah walked into the dining room near the kitchen and sat down in an office chair to read the letter while Jack and I sat on the opposing couch with his dogs between us. As Hannah read the letter, she sobbed. When she finished the letter, she held it to her bosom and said, "If I am going to sign off on this, then you are going to do this my way. I am not going to sign off unless Stan and Polly and Johan also sign off. But this time, if you are going to date one another, you are going to go back to start off just being friends. You are not going to talk to each other or see each other every day. You are going to do this my way." I remember thinking, "What the h-e-c-k?!" But Jack just nodded his head in agreement.

It was time for us to leave and go deliver the second letter to Polly and Johan. Jack went to use the bathroom while I walked into the kitchen to talk to Hannah. I mentioned to Hannah that she had a lot of responsibilities on her shoulders; she was the head of the household. Instead of hearing my words the way they were intended, still crying from the letter, she wheeled around and hissed at me, "Is this you trying to manipulate me?" I told her, "Ask God." When Jack came out of the restroom, I went in to use it. I noticed above the doorway that a steak knife was jammed in between the door molding and the wall. When I came out, I asked Hannah, "Why is there a knife in the bathroom?" She said, "Oh, we have knives in every room just in case someone breaks in, and we need to defend ourselves." I remember thinking that was craziness. Who has knives in every room? Who talks to their father this way and tells him that they are going to oversee their father's dating relationship? As we were leaving, both Jack's and my cell phones went off like popcorn with Polly and Johan telling us that we were not welcome to come and deliver the letter to their house because Stan had warned them that we were coming. Because of that, Jack drove me back to my home in Carlsbad.

He was so upset and rattled that I suggested that he pull to the side of the road and let me drive, which he did. When we got to my home, he was furious. I told him that I have five adult children, and over the years I have done all sorts of things to disappoint them, anger them, and sin against them. But not one of my five kids would ever consider talking to me or treating me the way his daughters treated him. They were treating him like he was a toddler. At my home, Jack, in his anger, decided that he was going to move out. He was going to get his motor home out of storage, find a park that would allow him to have dogs, and relocate somewhere close to where I was so we could spend time together. Once again, he proposed, saying that he wanted us to spend the rest of our lives together. We spent the next few hours talking about what life would be like for us. It was wonderful. Once again, my heart was full of affection for him with a new hope. Around nine o'clock Jack got a text from Hannah asking him when he planned to come home. I could not believe that he was letting his daughter demand a curfew, but he decided to go home and tell Hannah that he was moving out. We kissed goodbye, and I was hopeful of our future together.

Thirty minutes later he texted me that he had arrived home safely. And I texted back, "Thank you for letting me know." About an hour later I texted him and asked, "How did it go with Hannah?" About an hour after that text, I got this final guillotine to my heart.

Unexpectedly, only hours after our conversation about reuniting our lives together, Jack texted me, "This is the final time. You have manipulated me for the last time. It is over. Please do not call me or text me again." I cannot begin to describe the shock that I experienced with that text only hours after the time we had spent together planning our future.

I included this God story because I believe that God sent Jack into my life and that Jack was indeed a blessing to me. Yes, it ended in sadness and disappointment. However, Jack gifted me with many things. He was a kind and generous man. He helped me feel good about myself and realize that I had value. He helped me know that I could experience love again. It was beautiful being loved by Jack. Even though it didn't end the way I had hoped, Jack came alongside me to help me heal. Even though I was disappointed at how it ended, I am thankful to have been loved by him.

TAYLOR

In July 2018 my youngest son who was attending graduate school in Berkeley needed to relocate for a one-year internship in Johnson City, Tennessee. To move across the country from California to Tennessee, he recruited his brother to drive with him. When I heard that he was going to be leaving, I asked his wife if she wanted to schedule a time for us to get together during his time away. She told me that her mother, Sydney, was flying out from Nashville to spend the week with her while the brothers were driving together across the country. Sydney was a good friend and prayer partner, and I was happy to hear that she would be visiting during this time. They decided to come south to Carlsbad and have a day of fellowship with me at the beach. We enjoyed a build-your-own-sandwich lunch buffet, and then we packed up our sand chairs and beach umbrellas and walked across the street to spend the afternoon at the beach. The date was July 6, 2018.

We had gabbed over lunch, and we gabbed some more sitting under our beach umbrellas on the beach. Then we just relaxed and enjoyed sitting there listening to and watching the waves. There were a lot of people on the beach that day. I was looking at the ocean enjoying the sights, sounds, and smells when a pretty, young blonde approached me. She asked me if I would do her a favor. I responded, "That depends. What is the favor?" She told me that it was her twenty-fifth birthday, and she was having a crappy day. She said that she had just moved from southern Illinois, and she didn't know anybody. She was going through a divorce from a Marine at Camp Pendleton, and she had applied for a new job but didn't get it. Since it was her twenty-fifth birthday, she wanted to know if I would hold her cell phone and her keys while she ran into the ocean with her clothes on. I extended my hand to hold her phone and keys and nodded that I would, but I looked at my daughter-in-law and her mother, and they knew exactly what I was going to do next and the three of us broke out in a peppy song rendition of "Happy Birthday!"

Taylor shed a few tears and then ran into the ocean with her clothes on and came out, of course, dripping wet. As she walked up to me, I instructed her to blow off her pointer finger and enter my telephone number on her phone. After she plugged it in, I told her, "Now you have one new friend." Afterward, my daughter-in-law felt the Lord lead her to speak into Taylor's life, and her mother pulled Taylor aside and prayed with her. Now Taylor shared with me that the previous weekend, she had asked the chaplain at Camp Pendleton to baptize her, and he did. She was newly baptized with no church home. Without knowing that, I invited her to attend church with me the next Sunday, and she accepted. Taylor and I have developed a very special relationship. She has become an adopted daughter; she refers to herself as my *bonus* daughter. We text, talk, and see each other almost every week. She is on a journey both spiritually and physically. She is a Lyme disease survivor but still has ongoing symptoms and health issues that she struggles with.

It was merciful of the Lord to bring our lives together for a variety of reasons. In light of the many health challenges that I have worked through over the years, I have both an understanding and compassion for Taylor and all that she is going through. She is a sharp, smart, accomplished young woman who has done a lot of her own research, and people pay attention to her when she talks. We are a special support for one another.

No one can or will ever replace my biological daughters, but Taylor is a gift from God in my life. We have genuine love and affection for each other. When she was still living in California, she consistently called, texted, initiated getting together, and attended church with me. I believe that God intentionally gifted us with each other. There were hundreds of people on the beach that day. Why did Taylor approach *me*? I know the answer to that. It is because God orchestrated it. I experienced two devastating miscarriages—one before my youngest daughter was born and one after her. I know in my heart that the first miscarriage was a daughter, and I named her Rebekah. In my time with the Lord and my musings, I often thought that daughter, whom I lost to miscarriage, would have been close to Taylor's age. I am intentionally full of gratitude for having Taylor in my life.

GOD STORYS

CALABRIA

In September 2019, the Academy of Applied Myofunctional Sciences hosted its annual conference in Rome, Italy. I really wanted to attend, but I didn't think I could afford to. In December or January before the conference, I had decided to do some research on the expense before I made my decision whether to go. At that time, I found round-trip airfare from LAX to Rome, Italy, for $350. With that reasonable airfare price, I decided to go to the conference. I had many months to figure out how to pay for the airfare and the early bird registration before September. I knew from traveling in Italy before that I could travel very economically, either the same or less than I could in the US.

The conference was going to be held at the Angelicum in Rome. I contacted the Angelicum and talked with an English-speaking priest who was originally from Canada. He was very helpful in suggesting where to look for affordable accommodation near the Angelicum so that I could walk from my hotel room to the conference—just a block away. While I was booking my airline reservation and plotting the dates for departure and return, I knew the Lord was directing me to stay longer than the dates of the conference. When I asked the Lord, "How much longer?" He was very specific in directing me to stay an extra week and a day. I had no idea why I was staying the extra time, but I knew that I was supposed to.

Out of obedience, I booked my airline ticket factoring in the extra time. Friends and colleagues who were also attending the conference asked me why I was staying longer and what I was going to do. All I would tell them was, "I don't know; I will let you know when I know." As the time for the conference approached, I still did not know why I was staying longer or what I was going to do.

Two weeks before my departure, I felt directed to clean out the closet in my home. I had schlepped crates of papers and files with me with every move and had never found time to sort through them. It was annoying that I couldn't use the closet because it was piled with crates and boxes, none of which I had used in four years. The crates were heavy, and several of them were stacked one on top of another. Jack had helped me move them when we were dating. I lifted the lid off the top crate and very quickly went through all the files and disposed of most of them. Jack and I relocated the top crate and just as we were about to open the lid of the second crate, I instructed Jack, "Wait!" as I felt the Lord directing me to pray. God directed my prayer. I prayed, "Dear Lord, if I am supposed to find my family in Southern Italy, then please help me find the maps that my sister Rose gave me over twenty years ago, highlighting the villages where my family is from." Now, I had given no thought to doing this prior to that moment, but I knew the Lord was directing me to pray that prayer. Jack helped me remove the lid to the second crate and to his astonishment and mine, the first file in that crate held the maps that my sister had given me over twenty years before.

There were no names, addresses, or telephone numbers, just maps with highlighted names of villages. There was the highlighted village of Francica and then the highlighted village of Pizzoni. *Francica* is my maiden name.

I did not know what to do with these maps or what God intended for me to do, but as the time to leave for the conference approached, I decided to take the maps with me. When I got to Rome, I showed them to my friend Licia, who lived in Northern

Italy, enjoying dual citizenship with the US. When she saw the maps of the province in Southern Italy called Calabria, she told me that she would introduce me to Dr. Saccomanno, a doctor in Rome, who used to live in Calabria.

While I was at the conference, I met with Dr. Saccomanno more than once, and even though we didn't speak the same language, she gave me helpful instructions. She firmly directed me to go by train to Naples after the conference, then take a boat to Capri and a train to Lamezia, then rent a car and drive to Tropea and stay there two nights. I had no idea why she was so specific in her instructions. I prayed and asked the Lord if this was His will. I had no other plans or instructions, so I presumed this was what God wanted me to do. When I checked the train schedule, I discovered that it would be a seven-hour train ride from Rome to Lamezia. So, I asked Dr. Saccomanno if there was any reason why I couldn't just fly to Lamezia since airline tickets were about the same price, and I would get there in one hour instead of seven.

She said that was fine and that if I did not find my family, I could reverse the trip and spend time later in Capri and Naples. So with that, I booked an airline ticket and flew to Lamezia. When I got to Lamezia, I walked to the terminal across the parking lot to the car rentals and rented a small stick shift Fiat Panda. The young man behind the counter was very helpful; he spoke good English but was very curious as to what a senior American woman was doing in Calabria by herself. He was very bold to ask, "What are you doing here?"

The farther south, I went the nosier people were. When I tried to rent the car, I had issues with my credit card. The credit card company had frozen my card thinking that my account was undergoing fraud. So the young man was very helpful and patient while I called the credit card company to have my card reactivated. While I was waiting, I asked him about Calabria—what it was and what are Calabrians like. And he smiled and laughed and said,

"Ohhhh, Calabrians, they love to eat!" And I just howled laughing! Is that why I am the way I am? While I was on the phone with the credit card company, he went in the backroom and brought out a plate of food, including fried eggplant rolls; he was feeding me while I was on the phone with the credit card company. And I must say, the rolls were delicious. He gave me a map and instructions about how to get to Tropea from the airport, which was about a forty-five-minute drive. I reserved an Airbnb in Tropea for two nights as Dr. Saccomanno had recommended.

I found my Airbnb and was pleased with my selection. It was a four-plex unit that had four separate bedrooms with a shared kitchen and balcony with tables and chairs. I had one of the four units, and no one else was renting any of the other units, so I had the entire place to myself. There had been some misunderstanding with the owner, and instead of the Airbnb reserving two nights, they had only reserved one. So the owner suggested that instead of paying the Airbnb for a second night, I could just pay him directly in cash, which I did. However, when I asked the owner for a receipt for the cash, he became irate and was practically yelling at me berating Americans, and I found myself feeling uncomfortable around him, thinking this man knows that I am staying here by myself. I had one of two decisions to make, either back down and cower or rise up, in my Italian blood, and confront him. I chose the latter. In English, I raised *my* voice, telling him to back off, and it worked. He was irritated with me, and it was evident he did not like me, and I did not like him. As he left, he growled at me that I should expect the maid to come the next morning around ten. I replied to him that I did not need the maid. I was willing to make up my own bed and use the same towels more than once. For the rest of the day, I explored Tropea, which was an incredibly beautiful seaside town or village. Tropea was lovely. There were ancient cobblestone streets and stone stairways, which led to little stone-walled stores. One night, there was a nighttime farmers market with vendors who were roasting nuts and selling homemade goods. Tropea was beautiful and unique. I could see why Dr. Saccomanno had told me to stay there. It was a seaside resort village, and people came there from all over the world, but everywhere I went people were nosy, inquiring as to why I was there.

The next day as I was doing my quiet time, sitting out on the balcony alone, having a cup of hot tea, in my pj's when I was surprised and interrupted with the maid entering. She did not speak any English and, using Google Translate on my cell phone, I told her that I did not need to her services that day, and she was happy to not have to clean my room. But instead of leaving, she settled in and sat down at the table where I was sitting and began to interrogate me as to why I was there. I tried to explain to her that I was there to find my family, but she did not understand what I was trying to communicate. So, I went to my room and got the maps. I showed her the maps and simply said to her, "*mi familia,*" and she sort of understood and nodded her head and pointed to the highlighted villages and said to me, "*mi amigos.*" So, I realized that she was telling me that she had friends in the villages where my family lived. I thought about that for a few minutes, then I asked her if she would be willing to ask her friends if they knew my family. She didn't jump at the opportunity, but she was OK with it. So, she asked me my family name, and I gave her my maiden name, and I gave her the names of my grandfather and grandmother.

My grandfather had grown up in that region and had left to go to the United States to work and send money back home to his family. That evening, I received a WhatsApp communication from Maria, the maid, telling me in Italian, which I translated using Google Translate, that she had found my family. She had called Nicola, who had called Laura, who had called Rosella. The next day, which was the day I was planning to check out and go to an Airbnb near Pizzoni, the maid showed up and basically in a pantomime instructed me to pack my suitcase, put it in my car, and follow her.

I had a girlfriend and prayer partner who was very cautious and concerned saying that this whole plan reminded her of Liam Neeson's movie *Taken*, and she was concerned that the maid had bad intentions. The Lord directed me to follow Maria, and so I did. We drove for about forty-five minutes on narrow, windy mountain roads from Tropea to Vibo Valentia, where Maria lived with her husband and two daughters. On the way, she stopped at a roadside farm stand and purchased some food for lunch. She then had me follow her to her home where her daughters had made a homemade Italian lunch for all of us. I think they were intrigued at having an American in their home, and we all attempted to talk in two different languages.

After lunch we just sat around like we were having a siesta, and I was quite baffled as to what we were doing and when. After a couple of hours, Maria instructed me to get back into my car and to follow her. I followed her through the streets of Vibo Valentia in front of their hospital, which was on a busy street for a small Italian town. There was nowhere to park, and so Maria stopped in the middle of the street in front of the hospital and ushered me to park behind her. With our car doors open, we were standing in the street as other cars drove around us. Another small car pulled up behind me and did the same. Then out of the car came my cousin Rosella and her husband Bruno, whom I met for the very first time. Rosella and Bruno spoke no English, so again we pantomimed. They directed me to have Rosella get in the car with me, and Bruno drove off on his own. Maria and her daughter hugged me goodbye; I took the tree of life necklace, which I had purchased in Jerusalem, from around my neck and put it around Maria's neck as a thank you for all she had done to help me find my family. She was pleased. So, for the next thirty minutes Rosella pointed out where I should turn, and we soon arrived at their home in Pizzoni.

I was invited, rather expected, to stay with them, and I was delighted to do so. They had purchased some Italian pastries, and I was welcomed in their home for the first time with these pastries and a cup of their strong, thick cappuccino coffee. Within a short time, their son and daughter-in-law, Maurizio and Claudia, arrived and we continued to visit with each other. Later that evening Rosella's brother, Mario came, and I met my cousin Mario for the first time. Rosella and Mario's father was my grandfather's brother. My grandfather George was the oldest of eight, and he was the first to immigrate to the United States. Rosella and Mario's father stayed in Italy. Mario brought a black and white photograph with him to our first meeting, and I immediately recognized the photograph of my grandfather George and remembered when it was taken. In the photograph was my grandfather George with his cane; he had lost a leg and used a wooden leg and a cane to walk. To the right of my grandfather was my grandmother's sister Mary's husband, Pat Bello. To the left of my grandfather was my Aunt Dorothy who was my father's sister. There was a little girl in the lower left-hand corner of the black and white photograph, and Mario told me that picture was of me when I was three years old. I looked at that picture with total recognition. I immediately smiled, thought about my girlfriend who warned me about Liam Neeson and being taken and realized if that photograph was a picture of me, then this truly was my family. Later that night they wanted to take me out to dinner for a pizza at their favorite pizza parlor. We piled into two or three cars, caravanned to the pizza parlor where I was laughing at the name of the Italian pizza parlor that was called *C'est La Vie;* and it was a pizza parlor that did not serve wine. I got a real chuckle out of the whole eating experience. From the pizza parlor, we went to Mario and Teresa's home and had dessert and beverages, homemade Limoncello, and some other treats that were delicious.

I spent the week and the day with all my cousins and their son and daughter and really enjoyed getting to know them. They were delighted to meet me, and I was thrilled to meet them. Over the years, my sister Rose refused to give me any information about our family, either who they were or where they were located. I never really understood her withholding that information from me, but sadly it went along with her general attitude of hating me. Everyday Rosella and Bruno would take me on another field trip to another town. One day we went to a large flea market, and Rosella and I had fun shopping with the different vendors. I bought music CDs by Calabrian musicians and a pair of shoes.

The highlight of our field trips was to a church; I think it was in the city or town of Bruno. It was a beautiful old, ornate, Catholic church that had votive candles, statuary, and Catholic icons. No one else was in the church. We entered from the back, and I motioned to Rosella and Bruno that I wanted to go up front by myself and stay there for a few minutes. I felt the Lord drawing me, and I responded by walking up the center aisle to the front pew. As I walked down the center aisle, I saw there was a patch of clear glass in the floor; when I stopped and looked down through the glass, my soul was touched as I saw bones of the martyrs who had died in that location centuries before. I was moved with emotion. I went to the front of the church and prayed, and I felt a connection, a bond with those martyrs. During that time in prayer, the past and the present came together at the same moment; I could feel the presence of those saints, and I was moved to emotion at the privilege of being brought to that place. As a sat there praying and weeping, God impressed upon me that this was why he brought me to Southern Italy. Yes, to meet my family, but even more so to be in fellowship with my family, the martyred saints. It was such a moving and emotional time for me that even after we left the church and moved to our next location, I was still very emotional. The whole experience touched not just my heart, not just my mind, but it touched my soul. I had never had an experience like that before. I am not typically an experiential Christian, but I am thankful that God sent me to places where I could experience such things.

After a week and a day, my family drove me back to Lamezia airport where I flew to Rome and from Rome back to LAX. It was a wonderful God-venture. I don't know what I expected or if I had any expectations, but I was amazed at how much I was just like them. I look like them, I talk like them, I move my hands when I speak like them, I eat like them; I recognize myself in them. Since then, I occasionally get texts and photos from them. We are bonded, and we are family. In my quest over the past ten years for healing and growth, this God-venture of discovering my family has been a necessary and integral part of my journey. I am thankful that the Lord guided me and directed me to stay that extra week and a day. I am thankful that he directed me to pray and ask for the maps. I am thankful for Dr. Saccomanno's instructions. I am thankful for Maria's help in finding my family. I am utterly amazed!

WAIT

To complete our final divorce decree, my husband and I had to agree to and have a Marital Settlement Agreement notarized. In that agreement, we divided assets and debts equally. Unfortunately, we had way more debt than assets. I was given two debts to resolve, as was he. One was a credit card debt of about $24,000; I did not have $24,000 nor did I have the resources to make payments on that amount. I contacted the credit union that held the debt and informed them that all I had was $5,000. I asked whether they would accept that amount to satisfy the debt, explaining to them the situation that had arisen with our divorce and division of property.

Over a couple of years, I stayed in touch with them and kept them informed, but nothing in my financial situation changed. Time after time when I would take this debt to the Lord and ask Him how I could resolve this morally, ethically, and responsibly, He consistently, resoundingly impressed upon me to wait. I did not know what I was waiting for, but it was really apparent to me that I was supposed to wait. And so I did; I waited, I prayed, and I kept in touch with them. About five years ago, my account was transferred to a new representative who did not know my situation with the $5,000. When I spoke with her and reiterated the history of the debt and the account and the situation, she was very sympathetic. She said, "Just wait, hold on, and let me see what I can do. This debt has been on the books for a very long time." After a while she came back on the phone and said that she had run a formula and because of the length of time that the debt had been outstanding she was able to reduce the amount from $24,000 to $4,700 and change. She asked if I was able to pay that amount. I was surprised and thrilled. I said, "Yes, I was able to pay that amount to resolve the debt and that I felt morally responsible to resolve it."

When God kept telling me to wait, I did not know why I was waiting or what I was waiting for. Finally, the credit union issued me a letter stating that the payment had fulfilled the obligation! I marvel at His involvement in all the issues in my life, big and small. I am thankful to God for helping me to perceive His guidance and obey His directive.

CRASH

My friend Leilah is a dentist in El Cajon. Over the past five years, we have attended many courses and conferences together. She referred one of her dental patients to me for collaborative health care and myofunctional therapy. I suggested that I meet her for lunch to discuss the patient's case. She is a very busy doctor, and it was hard to coordinate our schedules, but we did. I agreed to drive to her office in El Cajon. Wouldn't you know that there would be a traffic accident on the freeway that day, causing me to arrive at her office quite late.

Leilah suggested that we walk across the street and have lunch at a nearby Mediterranean restaurant. We ordered a shared plate and began talking and collaborating. We were very involved in our conversation when we both heard the screeching of brakes. We looked up from our table through the front window of the restaurant, which was located on a street corner. We saw a white car swerving and being chased by three police cars. As the driver of the speeding white car attempted to make a left turn on the street in front of us, he missed the turn and drove right into the restaurant where we were sitting and eating. A huge explosion of noise and glass and building particles flew through the air. The noise was horrendous, both when the car crashed and when the driver backed out and took off, eluding the police. Leilah yelled for me to run leaving her purse behind.

We both ran out the back door not knowing if the building would collapse because its front wall had been demolished. Many people on the street and around the area were affected and traumatized by this horrendous crash. It was a miracle that no one had been run over in the process as there were pedestrians on the sidewalk in front of the restaurant. After several minutes, Leilah and I composed ourselves and evaluated the situation to see if it was safe to go back into the building so Leilah could get her purse. And we did. It was a disaster; there was glass everywhere. The wait staff was very shaken up. One woman who might have been the restaurant owner was distressed because she was planning to host a wedding reception there the next day. I made sure our lunch tab was paid and left a sizable tip behind.

If I had not been late for lunch that day, we would have been in the restaurant eating earlier with many other people. God did not specifically direct me that day, but I believe that my being late for lunch, due to the freeway traffic accident, was no coincidence. Looking back, if we had sat anywhere else in the restaurant, we could have been either injured or killed. For days after the crash, I experienced a mild form of PTSD, which affected my ability to sleep at night. Fortunately, God was merciful, and that was short-lived. My youngest son, the psychologist, recognized the symptoms and made recommendations for my recovery. God did not work in threes that time nor did I feel enveloped by the invisible cloud of the Holy Spirit. But I did feel loved and protected, and I know that God cares about all the small details in my life. He is a very personal God, and I covet the relationship that I have with Him.

THEODORE

The second time I attended the thirteen-week Divorce Care Bible Study, I was given a handout, which listed names and contact information for people who might be helpful for anyone going through a divorce. These were people that the church had vetted and felt confident referring us to use; the list included names and contact information for attorneys and real estate people. Through that list, I met Jerry, a financial planner, in the spring of 2018. Jerry was a Christian, and I appreciated his help with opening a Roth IRA. One morning in the fall of that year when Jack and I were experiencing the difficulties of breaking up repeatedly, I was awakened by one of my God Taps. God instructed me to go Jerry with Jack. That direction made no sense to me at all, but His prompting was unrelenting. Slightly embarrassed, I contacted Jerry and explained my experience to him. He told me, "You probably don't know this, but I am an ordained chaplain, and I have had special biblical training to counsel couples, especially couples who are older and who are in second relationships or marriages—widowed, divorced, and such. And I thought, "Oh, well now, that makes sense" because taking Jack to a financial planner had made no sense to me at all.

Jerry sent me an email with an attachment. At the time, I was doing a considerable amount of travel, and my schedule was remarkably busy. It took me a couple of weeks to open the attachment. But in the body of the email, Jerry said, "I usually give this in small chunks to my counselees, but here it is in its entirety." When I finally got around to opening the attachment I laughed out loud because Jerry had sent me forty-one questions. And of the forty-one questions, thirty were either the same or similar to the thirty questions that God had given me previously to give to Jack. So, with laughter, I knew why God had directed us to Jerry, and I was thankful that Jerry was biblically grounded in his counsel.

We were in Jerry's office seeking biblical counseling the second to the last time before Jack broke up with me. I was devastated and distressed. But I remember Jerry asking me toward the end of our time together whether I wanted to come back for biblical counseling by myself. I was a little taken aback by the question. I had not really given it any thought. It was all very new to me. I was already in therapy with a woman who specialized in helping to resolve past traumas. I did not know whether I wanted to go to two counselors at the same time even though they were for very different reasons. From my recollection, the next time I met with Jerry, he produced a sheet of paper with nine bullet points on it, listing areas in which he thought he could help me with biblical counseling. I do remember that this brought me to tears when I realized that, as a counselor, he had listened. I felt known and I felt cared for. I was pleased to be counseled from God's Word in those nine areas of personal challenges. Jerry asked if I minded if he took five minutes at the beginning of every counseling session to do a Bible study. I was thrilled with that. Jerry initiated our next session by doing a word study on Psalm 19, verses 7 through 9, and he created a three-page handout for us to use in our next several sessions. From the study of Psalm 19:7, Jerry guided a word study of the words *perfect* and *sure.* He explored God's definition of those words and shared that he had a particular annoyance when people used the word *perfect* for any other reason than in relationship to God. I had never heard that before, and I realized that I use the word *perfect* inappropriately much of the time.

The day of the "perfect" study was a very demanding and intensive day for me, and when I met with Jerry at the end of the day, I was exhausted. But I had never been very good at self-care, with boundaries or even listening to my body. So as I left Jerry's office feeling exhausted, instead of going straight home, I ran a few errands. The first was to return an item to a local grocery store. The second was a return to Fry's. As I was driving Palomar Airport Road to the coast to go home, I realized . . . "Oh no, I have to do a Lunch and Learn session tomorrow in San Diego." There were no restaurants or grocery stores near the dental office in San Diego. So in my exhausted state, I decided to go to Trader Joe's and pick up lunch for the staff for the next day. It was about eight in the evening, and Trader Joe's closes at nine. I needed five salads.

When I walked into the produce section, a young man was stocking the salad shelves. In my exhausted state, I asked him to give me five salads.

And he asked, "What kind do you want?"

I said, "I don't care."

He said, "Do you want five of the same salad, or do you want five different salads?"

And I responded, "I don't care." I was so depleted. So he put five different salads in my cart, and I proceeded to the checkout. I was not paying any attention to where I was, I just rolled my cart up to the checkout. I do remember in my robotic state that a young, tall dark-haired Caucasian man was working the cash register. I paid for the salads, and as I was walking out, I said, "I forgot water bottles."

Since no one was behind me in the checkout line, he offered to get the water bottles for me, which he did. When he put the case of water bottles in my cart, he asked me if they were the ones that I wanted, and I responded, "Perfect."

Now when I said that word, the young man said, "Oh, I love that word."

And I remember thinking, really? I said, "It's interesting to me that you would say that because I just left a Bible study where we were studying the word *perfect*."

And he said, "I believe in God. What did you learn about that word?"

I told him that I was in a Bible study with a chaplain named Jerry and that he had just recently told me that the word *perfect* should only be used when talking about God. The young man said he found that interesting and would like to talk about it some more. I thought about the Scripture verse for myself and in my level of fatigue *"When I am weak then I am strong"* (2 Corinthians 12:10). I was incapable of having a serious conversation with this young man at that time. The young man, Theodore, rang the bell so someone could help me load my water bottles into the car. I went home and went to bed.

The next day, I found myself in the San Marcos area again on Palomar Airport Road, which was not an area that I frequent often. As I was returning to my coastal home, God directed me to go back to Trader Joe's, impressing on me that I had unfinished business to take care of there. Since Theodore had mentioned that he would be interested in the word study, I decided to take him one of Chaplin Jerry's cards along with one of mine, so he had my contact information. When I got to Trader Joe's, just a little bit before two in the afternoon, the first thing I did was to scan all the registers to look for this young, tall, dark-haired white man. No one looked familiar. And then I started to doubt God's directing me to go there. I looked up over my right shoulder and said, "Why am I here? Did

I hear You right?" I started to leave, and then I remembered in just a few days I would need two or three additional items from Trader Joe's that I might as well get instead of waiting. So, I got a cart, went down the aisles, selected the items, put them in my cart, and proceeded to check out. I knew that I had not seen Theodore, so I didn't bother looking for him again. There was no one in line at the register where I chose to check out; that is why I selected it.

As I was checking out and rifling through my purse for my wallet to find my debit card, the male voice of the checker said to me, "Weren't you just here last night?" I looked up and honestly, I swear I had never seen that young man before in my life. I gave him a look of, "Was that you last night?" And he smiled his big smile and said, "You don't recognize me because I got my hair cut this morning." I thought to myself, "And did you also change your skin color since last night?" because Theodore was black. I thought, "How could I have been so tired to have missed that detail the night before?" Theodore was again very cheerful and helpful, and I offered to give him Jerry's card and my card for future contact. He was very appreciative and gracious and asked me, as I was leaving, if I would like to have his card too. Of course, I accepted it and was happy to have it.

Two or three days later, I received a text from Theodore saying that he had talked to his girlfriend about me and that they both would like to meet with me on Friday morning to talk. I asked Jerry if he was available to meet with us, but he was not. So, Theodore and Chelsea and I met for an hour and a half at Starbucks on Friday morning. They are both believers in God, and it seems that all three of us had been led to write a book. Chelsea is a poet and is in the process of writing and publishing her poetry. Theodore is a photographer and videographer and does beautiful work through the lens of a camera. For an hour and a half, we had a delightful time talking about our relationships with God. Theodore is on a journey like the one I have been on for these past five years, questioning things like denominational church affiliation. We had an enriching time, and I believe we will enjoy growing in our relationships in the future. I did tell Theodore when I was checking out the second time, I had looked for him and that he wasn't there. And he said, "Oh, I just came on at work at two in the afternoon. I just came at that time to be there for you."

He might have been kidding, but I knew it was not coincidental. Once again, God orchestrated the events to come together for our paths to cross. I do not know what God's intention is in the future for Theodore and Chelsea and me, but I do know that somehow the three of us are part of God's sovereign plan. I could have ignored His direction, His nudging to go back to Trader Joe's the second day. I am glad that I did not, and now have two new friends as a result of that obedience.

PREQUEL:
FRED AND MARILYN

When I was in high school in May 1970, I knew that I wanted to go into a health-care profession. When I graduated from high school, I was a National Honors Society member. I graduated with units from the local junior college, and I was awarded a scholarship to a two-year Medical Assisting program, which began in the fall.

Sometime that summer, I became ill as I frequently did with strep throat or tonsillitis. I drove myself to our family physician, Dr. Watson, who had been our family doctor since I was a small child. Because I was a long-standing patient, I was surprised when I encountered a new medical assistant. It was difficult to talk with my throat so badly infected, but I managed to ask questions. I asked her who she was, and how long she had been working there, I also told her of my intentions to begin a Medical Assisting program in the fall.

She was older than I was and very friendly and helpful. Despite my sore throat, I managed to ask her what kind of work she did before taking the job at my doctor's office. She told me that while she had been in medical assisting school, she had a weekend job working at Sherman Oaks Community Hospital as an EKG technician. I remember asking her, "What was an EKG technician?" She explained that EKG techs administer patients' electrocardiograms.

I had never heard of that before, so I knew nothing about it. We talked on and off before and after the appointment with Dr. Watson, and when I was leaving, she surprised me by making me an offer. She said, "Since you are starting Medical Assisting school in the fall, would you like to take over my weekend job as an EKG technician? I will train you." I considered her offer. And so, she did, and I did. I was working in a hospital laboratory at seventeen years of age. In those days, there was no formal training for an EKG technician; there was no certification, just on-the-job training. Not only was I responsible for administering the electrocardiograms, but I was also responsible for transcribing the readings that the cardiologists did while I was on my shift. I remember having to spell words like *Bradycardia* and *Tachycardia* and other terms related to cardiology that, prior to that, were unfamiliar to me. I really liked the job and felt privileged to have been offered it.

I had worked at Sherman Oaks Community Hospital for less than a month when the full-time EKG technician gave notice that she was pregnant and moving to Peoria. They immediately offered me her full-time job. It didn't make sense to me to go to medical assisting school, when I now had a full-time job doing something in health care that I really enjoyed. So, I gave up my scholarship and accepted the full-time position. I had two bosses, Luisa and Fred. Fred was married to Marilyn. In the laboratory where I worked, Karen, the receptionist, was married to Steve, and Mary the RN phlebotomist, was married to Huey. All seven of us became very close friends.

As my boss, Fred, was always looking out for me; it was like having a big brother at work overseeing me. One day, Fred suggested that we have lunch together in the hospital cafeteria.

Over lunch he asked me, basically, "What do you want to be when you grow up?"

I remarked, "What do you mean? I'm already an EKG technician."

He said, "No, you need to go back to college and get a degree in another health-care profession."

I shrugged my shoulders and said, "Well, I already make $350 a month. Why do I need to do that?"

Like a good big brother, he said, "You just have to." So, he asked me what I thought I wanted to be.

I started listing health-care professions, starting with nursing. Then Fred proceeded to tell me all the reasons why I didn't want to be a nurse.

I suggested an X-ray tech, and he told me why I didn't want to be an X-ray tech.

And then I suggested a lab tech like himself, and he told me all the reasons why I did not want to be a lab tech.

After exhausting my list, I got frustrated with him and said, "OK, you're so smart. What do you think I should be?"

And he said, "I think you should be a dental hygienist."

I responded with, "What's that?" And he informed me, "That's the person in the dental office who cleans your teeth."

I remember saying to him, "Eww, yuck! That's so gross!"

Then he said, "They earn over a hundred dollars a day!"

Fred's wife Marilyn was a dental hygienist, and she had several years of an outstanding dental hygiene career. Fred was persuasive, and I began my quest to research and apply to dental hygiene schools.

Now as an aside, I might mention that while I was working on a random Saturday, I was approached by a process server at work, who inquired as to whether I was Victorya. I acknowledged that I was, and he served me with papers! My dad was taking me to Superior Court to legally emancipate me—to legally disown me. At the time I was eighteen years of age, but the legal age in California was twenty-one. My dad was no longer willing to pay child support to my mother for my living expenses even though I was still living at home at the time. Being served with those papers at work was traumatic, and trying to comprehend that my dad was legally disowning me was incredibly painful. But Fred was there to help me through that very difficult and harrowing time. My dad was successful through the court system at disowning me.

At the time, there were only three schools in the State of California that taught dental hygiene and graduated dental hygienists: the University of the Pacific in San Francisco, USC in Los Angeles, and Loma Linda University in Loma Linda, California. All those schools charged very expensive tuition, and I was not able to meet that tuition obligation. But since there was an immense shortage of dental hygienists in 1970, the State of California funded three junior colleges to open up dental hygiene programs. It was an expensive application process, with hundreds of applicants. I applied to two junior colleges and was accepted to both. I decided not to go to Cerritos because it was too far away; I was accepted to Pasadena City College as an alternate student.

I was told there were 800 applicants, and the school was only accepting eighteen. I was number nineteen on the list; one of the eighteen dropped out to become an airline stewardess instead, so I was offered the last opening in the 1971 dental hygiene program. One of the prerequisites was a passing grade in college organic chemistry. I had taken that course as a high school student at the local junior college, but I did not get a good grade in it. My chemistry teacher at the time knew I understood the material, but I did not test well. He agreed to give me a passing grade if I promised to retake chemistry in summer school. So, I was enrolled in the summer school chemistry class when I was summoned by the Dean of Pasadena City College. When I was in his office, he informed me that they had mistakenly admitted me and that because my parents did not live in the Pasadena school district, I was not going to be able to attend in that district. He gave me a certain amount of time, if I remember correctly about two weeks, to overcome this challenge.

My options were to (1) have one of my parents move to the Pasadena school district as a permanent resident: (2) find a man to marry me, which would then make me independent: or (3) find someone twenty-one or older to be my legal guardian. I had already been legally emancipated because my father had disowned me. However, Pasadena City College would not accept that.

In my chemistry class, there was a student who was recruiting members for a service club on campus called The Adelphians. When she approached me for membership, I asked her if she had an older sister, and she said yes. I negotiated with her that if she could convince her older sister who was twenty-one to be my legal guardian, then I would join her club. She did, and I did.

On the last day of my deadline, my mother and I went to court on a Friday afternoon to have this nameless twenty-one-year-old assigned as my legal guardian. I do not remember her face or her name. But her willingness to help me allowed me to enter dental hygiene school.

The two-year dental hygiene program was an intensive that prepared us to sit for our State and National Boards. We were prepared so well that our graduation class ranked in the 97th percentile of all US students taking the boards that year.

In all my years as a dental hygienist, the most dramatic series of events occurred in one day; these events have influenced the rest of my life. In a single day, I had five (out of twelve) dental patients boldly and bluntly ask me if I had a personal relationship with Jesus Christ. Finally, another dental patient, Del, invited me to church. In all my years as a dental hygienist, I do not recall anyone else asking me that question. I did end up going to church with Del and her husband after a particularly difficult week. It was at that church service in Pasadena that I accepted and invited Jesus Christ to be my Lord and Savior. My relationship with Him began to grow after that day of unique encounters.

I ended my traditional dental hygiene career of forty-four years in 2017. I enjoyed that profession immensely and became passionate about patient education. Fred's intentional involvement and encouragement in my life led me down a fulfilling professional path. His wife Marilyn became one of my very best friends and faithful prayer partners. Fred and Marilyn have passed on to be with God forever in eternity.

I did not recognize God's leading or involvement in my life then, but I do now. He connected the dots. I now know that He was involved in guiding me through those times.

WHY VICTORYA?

My parents were children of Italian and German immigrants. Childhood was a difficult and confusing formative season. Early on in my childhood, God was with me and in me, and I sensed His presence. I am at a place now where I can express gratitude for the journey of trials and tribulations because they are part of "my" story, and they contributed to forming me into who I am today. I was born on July 27, 1952. On my birth certificate, my name is "Victoria." For most of my life, I was called by my nickname, Vickie. About ten years ago I decided to be called by my birth name, Victoria.

I've been very aware of God's intentional involvement in my life; I am full of gratitude for the intimate relationship that I have with my Creator. I don't enjoy trials and suffering, but I do appreciate their purpose. I see evidence in my life of how they have helped to transform me and mold and shape me into being more like Him.

In the past year, I have decided to legally change the spelling of my name to reflect my victory over adversity... my *victory* in Christ. As a young child, my parents told me that I was named Victoria for a few reasons. First, since they were practicing Catholics, Our Lady of Victory was my designated patron saint. Second, they told me that my birthday coincided with the day that the United States victoriously won the Korean War. As I have previously mentioned, my birth was dramatic. I was a full-term, undiagnosed, placenta previa who suffocated in my mother's birth canal and needed to be resuscitated after an emergency C-section. As a toddler, I was diagnosed with 30 percent club feet on both of my legs, and for a few years, I had to wear casts and braces on my legs. My mother told me that I learned to walk in those braces, and when they were finally removed, I had to learn how to walk all over again.

My legacy is Victory! My beautiful, glorious life has been punctuated with adversity since I took my first breath. I now daily experience my victory over adversity through Christ. I want to meditate on that, remember it, and be aware of it as frequently and as often as when I see and sign my name. So, I have chosen to change the spelling of my name to "Victorya."

The song, "Goodness of God," by Jenn Johnson resonates with me . . . you might appreciate it too!

Soli Deo Gloria—To God be the Glory.

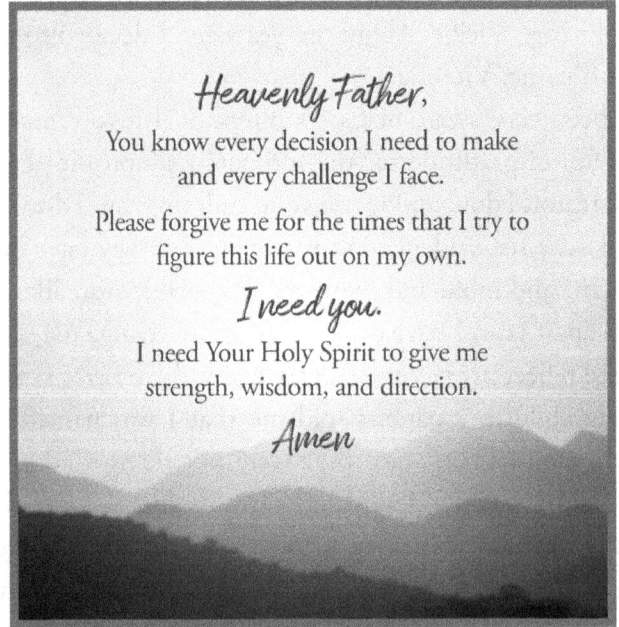

Heavenly Father,
You know every decision I need to make and every challenge I face.
Please forgive me for the times that I try to figure this life out on my own.
I need you.
I need Your Holy Spirit to give me strength, wisdom, and direction.
Amen

ENDNOTES

1. Leslie Brandt, *Psalms Now* (Concordia Publishing House, Revised 1996).
2. Larry Crabb, Don Michael Hudson, and Al Andrews, *The Silence of Adam: Becoming Men of Courage in a World of Chaos* (Zondervan, 1995).

www.ingramcontent.com/pod-product-compliance
Lightning Source LLC
Chambersburg PA
CBHW060520090426
42735CB00011B/2307